Building Great Relationships
All about emotional intelligence

By the same Author

The Joy of Living with Yoga

Effective Yoga

Retired but not Tired

Back to Nature

Building Great Relationships
All about emotional intelligence

B K Trehan, M.Tech.
with
Indu Trehan, M.Sc.

Sterling Paperbacks

STERLING PAPERBACKS
An imprint of
Sterling Publishers (P) Ltd.
A-59, Okhla Industrial Area, Phase-II, New Delhi-110020.
Tel: 26387070, 26386209; Fax: 91-11-26383788
E-mail: mail@sterlingpublishers.com
www.sterlingpublishers.com

Building Great Relationships
© 2010, B K Trehan with Indu Trehan
ISBN 978 81 207 4923 8

All rights are reserved.
No part of this publication may be reproduced, stored in a retrieval system or transmitted, in any form or by any means, mechanical, photocopying, recording or otherwise, without prior written permission of the author.

Printed in India
Printed and Published by Sterling Publishers Pvt. Ltd., New Delhi-110 020.

Acknowledgements

I am greatly indebted to my wife Indu, who is not only the coauthor of the book, but also a beacon in my life. She has given me tremendous support all through our long married life, in spite of my occasional faulting.

I also owe my gratitude to all our friends and relatives, especially Vijay Khokha, AP Chaudhri, Bharti Desai, Sudhir Aggarwal, Om, Amit, and Nikita Banga for their wonderful, inspiring 'e-mail forwards', some of which have been used in the book. We hope the book will take these beautiful, life transforming e-mails to a large number of readers, not only to five-ten as requested by senders of some of these mails.

I am also grateful to the wise, great people of the present and the past whose quotations we have freely used in the book to stress our viewpoints. As the great British Prime Minister Disraeli rightly said, "The wisdom of the wise and the experience of the ages are perpetuated by quotations."

I am thankful to Sterling Publishers Private Limited for publishing this book. I hope the book will kindle the fire of love and compassion among the readers and help them to create great relationships.

And finally, I pay my gratitude to late Mrs. Prakashwanti Trehan, who was not only my mother, but also a spiritual guru. She helped me to deepen my faith in God and His myriad creation. Loving, understanding, caring, compassionate and benevolent, she was my role model of an ideal relationship. With great humility, I dedicate this book to her.

bktrehan@yahoo.co.in **B K Trehan**

Contents

Acknowledgements	v
Introduction	1

1. **Basics of Relationships** — 6
   • Chemistry of Relationships • Love Springs from the Heart • Heart is Our Soul • Loving Heart and Thinking Mind • Relationship Triangle

2. **Nurturing Relationships** — 17
   • Living by heart • Prayer • Silence and Solitude • Meditation • Yoga • Deep Mindful Breathing • Yoganidra • Rituals and Traditions • Building Great Relationships

3. **Relating to Your Own Self** — 38
   • Know Thyself • Love Yourself • Self-care of Body • Where Are You Going? • The Comedian Inside You • Don't Worry What Others Say • Don't judge Others, Judge Yourself • Tap Your Inner Resources

4. **Marrying Forever** — 58
   • Troubled Marriages • Finding a Perfect Partner • Mantras of a Successful Marriage • Love Your Partner • Respect and Appreciate Your Partner • Trust Your Partner • Don't Criticise or Blame Your Partner • Balance Your Family Life • Handle Disagreements Gracefully • Make Mutual Adjustments • Honour Your Commitments • Share with Your Partner • Grow with Your Partner • Think Before Breaking Up

5. **Art of Parenting** 86
   • Love Your Children • Know Your Children's Needs • Be Patient with Children • Disciplining Children • Inculcate Values • Walk the Talk • Handling Teenagers • Handling Adult Children • Grand Parenting

6. **Dealing With Your Parents** 105
   • Coming to Terms • Love and Respect Your Parents • Being Grateful to Your Parents • Bridging the Generation Gap • Caring for Older Parents • Eyeing on Parent's Property

7. **Friends are a Treasure to Keep** 120
   • Who is a True Friend? • Be Worthy of Your Friends • Equality in Friendship • You Can't Have Too Many Friends • Be Supportive of Your Friends • Sacrificing for Friends • Friends and Money Matters • Life is Fun with Friends • Friendship Day • Your Extended Relationships

8. **Relationships at Workplace** 142
   • Workplace is a Family • Work is Worship • Love Your Work • Maintain Good Communications • Nurture Teamwork • Establish Realistic Work Standards • Balancing Work and Family • Handling Workplace Stress

9. **Relationship with God** 163
   • God Does Exist • Your Relationship with God • Deepen Your Faith • Trust in God • Loving God • Be Humble, Don't Challenge God • Thank God for His Blessings

   Bibliography 184

Introduction

Our greatest joy and our greatest pain
comes in our relationships with others

Stephen R. Covey

Why this book? In one of our earlier books, *Retired, But Not Tired*, we had devoted one chapter to 'Family and Friends' in which we briefly described the importance of having relationships in one's silver years. The book received great appreciation from the readers, and some even suggested we write a full volume on this vital subject to help millions of people around the world to improve their troubled relationships.

We agreed to our readers' suggestion, and set to reflect on the subject of relationships more deeply. We realised that relationships are not only limited to our intimate loved ones but involve everybody in the family, society, business and elsewhere whose support and companionship we need to keep us going in life. And we need them not only when we are old, but at every stage of life, more so when we are young and inexperienced in facing the challenges of everyday life.

Relationships connect us to others, and make us happy and whole. Albert Einstein summed up relationships as: "A human being is a part of the whole called by us 'Universe', a part limited in time and space. We experience ourselves, our thoughts and feelings, as something separate from the rest. This delusion is a kind of prison for us, restricting us to our personal desires and affection for a few persons nearest to us. Our task must be to free ourselves from the prison by widening our circle of compassion to embrace all living creatures and whole of nature in its beauty."

In our quest to understand the secrets of great relationships, we studied the lives of a number of people known to us, some very closely, some remotely, and our own personal experience of handling relationships at home, work and community for over six decades. Some of these were highly successful stories while others were big disasters. We realised that in all these stories, there was one thing in common that held people together in relationships, and its absence tore them apart.

What is that which bonds us together in relationships? Money, power, position, status, beauty, knowledge, name or fame! No, none of these! Ask those who have troubled relationships. If money made great relationships, Ratan Tata, and for that reason so many other billionaires in the world, would not have remained single. If position or status could hold people together, French President Nicolas Sarkozy would have not had two divorces before marrying Carla Bruni. If beauty attracted partners in relationships, Heather Mills, the British screen icon and pop star Paul McCartney would not have broken apart. Or Marilyn Monroe, the Hollywood beauty of yesteryears would not have been divorced twice. Likewise, if fame were able to create great relationships, the famous author Sir Salman Rushdie would not have four divorces. In the same tone, if position, power, name or fame could win friends, former US president George Bush and late Sadam Hussain would have been great friends and not at war with one another.

Time and again people have achieved all the above things, yet they ended up in unhappy relationships. What then, makes great relationships? Should we tell you? It is the four-letter word, 'LOVE'. Yes, it is the deep feeling of love, which like a powerful magnet attracts one to another in a relationship. It is the profound love for each other that keeps us together as a husband, wife, father, mother, son, daughter, friend, neighbour, colleague, or the man at the counter. The feeling that we are loved, are lovable and capable of loving attracts us to others in great relationships and provides a sense of fullness in life. And it is the abundance or lack of love and affection that creates or ruins a great relationship. In fact, discovering that love within us, and connecting with someone else is just a part of life's basic needs that must be fulfilled. Otherwise we are not complete.

Someone expressed the importance of love in life in this way: "What is success if, when you're standing at the top, having achieved everything you wanted to achieve, you have no one to share it with? Make love your number one aim. Love is your greatest possibility in the one life you have to live."

Building great relationships is all about understanding the mechanics of love, which is the cornerstone of all relationships. But where we often seem to go wrong is in understanding the mechanics of love itself. Because we associate love to only mind or brain, we consider the whole concept of relationships as a matter of intellect, reasoning and imagination. However, this is not true. If love were a product of brain or intellect only, the more educated, learned urban people would have been perfect husbands or wives, parents, bosses, colleagues, friends or others; and the ordinary village folks would have trouble relating to others. In the same token, psychologists, the people who understand mind better than any one else, would probably be highly successful with their own relationships. In reality, however, we have comparatively more cases of broken marriage, divorce, trouble with parents and children, and dubious friendship among the more educated and scholarly people.

Remember, love is not a matter of head only. In fact, love is more a function of heart than the head. Love is a feeling, an emotion, which springs from deep inside our heart, the place where our spirit or soul resides. Love is that subtle energy generated in the heart or soul that attracts and connects us to others. Our analytical, reasoning brain cannot define completely the amazing power of love, and yet when we are in love our heart understands it fully.

Quite often in relationships, we start out full of thrill and promises, and every moment we spend together feels wonderful. But as time passes, the sheen of relationships fades away. We have other commitments and priorities – careers to manage, children to raise, people to meet, and places to visit. The hurry and glamour of present day life often distracts us from our near and dear ones. The challenges and stresses we face today interfere with our relationships. We require right attitude, priorities and actions to remain deeply connected with those who matter the most in our life.

When your relationships start crashing, you wonder what happened. You wish you knew how to set things right. But you are helpless, and look for help. Where do you go? *Building Great Relationships* will guide you how to create relationships, be they your spouse, children, parents, in-laws, friends, clients, bosses, co-workers, or others who are important to us. No matter what kind of relationship you are involved in, it takes two to work it properly as nothing in the world is one-sided. You need to do your part and learn how to make your relationship great and keep it great.

Most principles and practices given in the book are based on ancient scriptures, advices and traditions, which, perhaps, got neglected and forgotten along the way to the present-day modernization. These principles are eternal and as relevant today as they were in earlier times. But the present day materialistic world, devoid of spirituality, has blinded our vision to apply them in our everyday life. If you apply these simple, yet powerful principles into your life, not only will you create loving relationships, you will have tremendous peace and joy in your life.

Introduction

We have written this book, not because we are great psychologists, or celebrity writers (we are not), but because we love you and want to share with you a few lifetime experiences - some happy and uplifting, and some unhappy and frustrating, that taught us and many others the art and science of making great relationships. Hope these will help you too, to bring a new meaning to your relationship, if you have been going through a rough time.

Frankly speaking, writing this book together has been a great experience and personal renaissance for both of us. Little did we know when we started working on the book that it would be our own awakening and transformation? Each time we sat down to reflect or scribble a few lines, our mind reflected upon the shortcomings of our own married life of nearly four decades, and the way we behaved and interacted with other family members, friends and coworkers. Many times we felt inadequate and failing ourselves in practising sincerely some of the concepts advised in the book. We tried to improve, but it takes time to change. If we were to get another life to live, and start a fresh, we will try to build perfect relationships practising genuinely the advice given in the book.

Building Great Relationships is the fifth in the series of books on life improvement topics we intend to write together in our retirement. The four already published include *The Joy of Living with Yoga*, *Retired but not Tired*, *Back to Nature*, and *Effective Yoga*.

We enjoyed writing this book and hope you not only like reading it but, find it useful for creating and maintaining great relationships. We will consider ourselves amply rewarded if even a very small percentage of millions of troubled relationships around the world could be mended through the help of this book.

God bless you.

1

Basics of Relationships

>Wisdom tells me I am nothing.
>Love tells me I am everything.
>Between the two, my life flows.
>
>*Nisargadatta Maharaj*

Man is not an island. He is a social being who needs the company and support of others to live. Living happily requires interacting with all those we are involved with - spouse, children, parents, other family members, friends, boss, coworkers, and people in the street. They all support us and make our lives meaningful. And oh yes! We almost forgot God who gives us the biggest support.

We interact with others through relationships. Relating to others who keep us going in life is a basic human need, we all strive for. We are inherently connected with all other beings in this large, worldwide human family here on earth. As a ripple effect, anything we do affects not only those immediately in our lives, but all other life on earth. The same is true for our relationships.

Relationships are necessary for life, health and growth. A stable happy relationship not only enriches your own life, but its positive influence reaches out to nurture humanity and all other beings on this planet. Healthy relationships offer unlimited opportunities for support, giving, receiving, sharing, growing and bringing purpose in life. Relationships are precious gifts that bring joy in our lives. They are great learning experiences, which inspire us to know who we are.

A great relationship is the bliss to be experienced in the calm and peaceful morning, to a productive workday, to a relaxing evening, and into a sound refreshing sleep in the night, day after day. Conversely, life becomes horrible when we have problems in relating to others. Wrecked marriage, broken family, ill health, career setback or loss of job, friends turning foes, loneliness, loss of esteem in society, disoriented life, frustration and depression are all products of stormy relationships. An unhealthy relationship is a curse that ruins one's life.

Chemistry of Relationships

Volumes have been written on how to make great relationships, yet somehow relationship problem still remains a major cause of human suffering. Ever increasing divorce suits, sexual harassment, discrimination, juvenile crimes, heinous murders, indiscriminate firing of innocent people, violence, terrorism, industrial strikes and layoffs that cause huge loss of jobs and money, and so on are all relationship problems at home, workplace or community.

Have you ever thought seriously why we have relationship problems? Perhaps not! We have relationship problems because we have not understood the very basics of what makes great relationships. Though we are all so much an active part of one or the other relationship, we spend so little a time in understanding the dynamics of what makes them work. Before we can be successful in building great relationships, it is necessary to broaden our understanding of how they work, what they mean and what we can do to enhance them.

As mentioned earlier in the previous chapter, it is not only the intellect, reasoning or logic, the products of our brain that build a relationship. Relating with wife, husband, children, parents, friends, co-workers, or whomsoever, does not mean demanding, dominating, convincing, coercing, manipulating, seducing or controlling them as most people do, to satisfy their own egos or whims. Relationships, on the contrary, are built on love and care for one another. "The unity that binds us all together, that makes this earth a family, and all men brothers and sons of God, is love. That love can take many forms," said Thomas Wolfe, the famous American writer. It may be the love of family and friends, the love between men and women, love of God, the love of country, the love of nature, and the love of all humanity. Love is the corner stone of all relationships.

> The best relationship is one in which your love for each other exceeds your needs for each other.

Love takes you from self-centeredness and selfishness to increased awareness and concern, to feelings of compassion and connection for others. Love is the experience of giving and receiving the joy of a shared life. It is deeply gratifying to feel loved, and to be able to love someone. "We need four hugs a day for survival. We need eight hugs a day for maintenance. We need 12 hugs a day for growth," said Virginia Satir, the noted American author and psychotherapist.

Unless love becomes a part and parcel of our way of life, we will not feel fulfilled in our relationships and life. "Love and kindness are the very basis of society. If we lose these feelings, society will face tremendous difficulties; the survival of humanity will be endangered," says The Dalai Lama. Today the world is suffering more from the hunger of love than the hunger of bread. This hunger of love must be satisfied to sustain relationships. As Mother Teresa had put it, "There is a terrible hunger for love. We all experience that in our lives - the pain, the loneliness. We must have the courage to recognize it. The poor you may have right in your family. Find them. Love them."

Love is the foundation of all relationships, and you know what happens when the foundation of a building is weak. Building a great relationship is like building a house on a strong foundation of love with compassion, respect, forgiveness, tolerance, gratitude, kindness, generosity, etc., as the other building blocks, which are all but different expressions of love only. The process of building the edifice of relationships is the same irrespective of relationship you are in. How you handle your woman or man is also how you handle a teenager son or a daughter, and how you handle your parents, and how you handle a customer, how you handle a business partner, and finally, how you handle any relationship indeed. As someone has said rightly, "There is only one sort of love, but there are a thousand copies."

Love has many names and forms. The love of a mother for her child is different from the love for her husband. A friend's love is different from the love of a romantic lover for his passionate beloved. And to 'Sir with love' from a student is altogether a different story. However, the common thread in each of these forms of love is the force that unifies, and overcomes separation. Though English language is restricted in its usage of the word 'love', Sanskrit has different names to express one's love for different relationships. Love for your beloved husband or wife is called *prem*, *vatsalay* is love for children, and *sneh* is used for friends and others. Love for God is called *bhakti*, devotion. Is it not interesting that this small four-letter word, 'love' in its different expressions has the power of bonding the entire world together in wonderful relationships?

Love Springs from the Heart

Love and its various expressions - compassion, gratitude, forgiveness, tolerance, etc. are all positive emotions or feelings that spring from the heart. It is your heart that swells or melts with love, that feels compassion and gratitude, that bursts or overwhelms with joy, and that breaks or feels heavy with the loss of a loved one. Love is like the wind. We cannot see it or grasp it. But we can experience it deep in our hearts as compassionate touch, affectionate words, an innocent smile, an understanding look, a shared moment or an act of kindness. You can feel love's power when you breast-feed your infant, look at your child playing, gaze at innocent wrinkled face of your grandmother or grandfather, or recall a cherished occasion you shared with your family.

Also from the same heart, arise negative emotions like, anger, hatred, jealousy, selfishness, ego, greed, lust, fear, and others, which are destructive, and play havoc in relationships. Building great relationships involves nurturing positive emotions, and getting rid of the negative ones. Unless we control our emotions, our relationships will keep suffering.

How do we control our emotions? First of all, we must understand that emotions are basically a function of our heart and not the head. It is the nature of heart to feel or emote, the nature of head is to think and analyze. While brain uses its rational and reasoning power to deal with people, through our heart, we access them trans-rationally, using instinct and intuition. Heart wisdom is therefore different from head knowledge. For loving relationships to flourish, the head and heart must function in harmony. In other words, we live a full and complete life, thinking with our heads but loving from our hearts. The secret of life and relationships is our heart, of which we know very little. A biblical story goes like this:

As the Lord was creating the world he called upon his archangels. The Lord asked his archangels to help him decide where to put the secret of life.

"Bury it in the ground," one angel replied.
"Put it on the bottom of the sea," said another.

"Hide it in the mountains," another suggested.
The Lord replied, "If I see to do any of those only a few will find the secret of life. The secret of life must be accessible to everyone!"
One angel replied, "I know; put it in each man's heart. Nobody will think to look there."
"Yes!" said the Lord, "Within each man's heart."

Heart is Our Soul

When we talk of heart, we generally refer to our physical heart, the mechanical pump that circulates blood throughout our body. This fist-size organ is, however, too small to contain our emotions or feelings, which are so profound and overwhelming. It is your emotional heart, your deepest self, soul or spirit located in the center of the chest cavity that circulates love in your entire being. For loving relationships to blossom, we must expand, purify and train our emotional heart and be wholehearted. It is this heart which is used a lot by spiritual seekers to develop emotions and intuitive capacity.

Purification of heart means opening, softening one's heart for others, expanding one's conscience, and developing a sense of unity of creation. As long as the heart is blocked, there is a sense of separation and alienation from others. When the heart is soft, open and flowing, you feel connected at a deep level of your soul to all the beings in your life. This feeling gives us the ability to see our own reflection in others. We see oneness of soul, spirit or God in everybody. This feeling of unity is so expansive and spiritual that we start looking the whole humanity as one, and the feeling of duality vanishes. When we feel the same Self, God or spirit in everyone, then who is the subject of our hate? Whom are we going to condemn or forsake? No soul remains our enemy, all are lovable. This feeling of universal love is beautifully expressed in verse 4.5 of the *Brihardaranyaka Upnishad* (translation from *Eknath Eshwaran*):

A wife loves her husband not for his own sake,
but because the Self lives in him.
A husband loves his wife not for her own sake,
but because the Self lives in her.

Children are loved not for their own sake,
but because the Self lives in them.
Wealth is loved not for its own sake,
but because the Self lives in it.
The Universe is loved not for its own sake,
but because the Self lives in it.

The Gods are loved not for their own sake,
but because the Self lives in them.
Creatures are loved not for their own sake,
but because the Self lives in them.
Everything is loved not for its own sake,
but because the Self lives in it.

> 'The person who loves others will also be loved in return.'
>
> God might be trying to work in another person's life through you.

When you start realising the presence of the universal self or spirit in your husband, wife, parents, children and others, your relationships with them will be transformed overnight. As the author and speaker, Paul Pearsall writes beautifully: "The path to paradise and the gate to heaven are through heart, and by having a warm, open heart, we allow God's love to happen to us. It is at these times, when we are most loving and ready to receive another heart."

Loving Heart and Thinking Mind

Our forebears knew that our heart has a powerful spiritual energy and deep wisdom with which it not only feels and loves, but also thinks, remembers and communicates with other hearts. The brain, they knew, is ill-equipped to translate the subtle nature of our feelings. However, as the modern society developed its brain it began to lose sight of its heart. We are overly consumed with production, efficiency, informatics, and problem solving by relying mainly on the cognitive and analytical skills of our brain with no regard to the power and wisdom of the heart. The rational brilliance of our brain has made us 'heartless'. "There is little or no communication between hearts, there is no sharing. Having lost contact with each other's hearts, we become isolated. We need to reinforce the links," says Ammachi Amritanandamayi, the noted spiritual teacher.

Further, the rational, modern industrialised society puts a lot of emphasis on individuality, personhood where each person's goals, performance, accountability, rewards, and penalties are the main focus. This philosophy is again brain driven. A person working exclusively from the brain, thinks of his own personal interests, how to compete, how to self-protect, how to push others away to become the best, and so on. There is no team-spirit and sense of fellow-feeling.

Although this philosophy of working exclusively from the brain has resulted in many exciting developments in the last few decades, it has shutdown our heart completely, killed our feelings, and played havoc on our personal lives and relationships. Handling people always with reasoning, rational and analytical power of the mind with no regard to the subtle power of the heart's love, instinct and intuition, is the main cause of our relationship problems today, may these be with spouse, parents, children, friends or co-workers.

In his best selling book, *Loving Each Other*, the noted Italian writer, Leo Buscaglia says, "we are far too rational in our relationships, far too ordered, organized and predictable. We need to find a place, just this side of madness and irrationality, where we can, from time to time, leave the mundane and move into spontaneity and serendipity, a level that includes a greater sense of freedom and risk – an active environment full of surprises which encourages a sense of wonder. Here, ideas and feelings, which would otherwise be difficult to state, can be expressed freely. A bond of love is easy to find in an environment of joy. When we laugh together we bypass reason and logic as the clown does. We speak a universal language – we feel closer to one another."

There is a humorous story about a great scientist who was absorbed in analysing things in his laboratory that he forgot his food and his other commitments at home. His wife tried to shake him from that state. She talked to him and when he did not attend to her, she started weeping. The scientist looked at her eyes filled with tears and said that he didn't understand why they were there. He then started to collect her tears to perform a chemical analysis of them.

That is what happens in relationships when there is just intellect and no feeling. In the words of yoga guru BKS Iyengar: "An intellectual mind that is unconnected to the heart is an uncultivated mind." Scientists tell us that we use only two per cent of the brain power available to us. Thank God! Imagine what would happen to our relationships if we started using the full potential of our brain!

The mystic poet and philosopher, Kahlil Gibran describes beautifully the conflict between the head and heart this way: Of All people you are the nearest to my soul, and the nearest to my heart; and our souls and hearts have never quarreled. Only our thoughts have quarreled, and thought is acquired, it is derived from the environment, from what we see in front of us, from what each day brings to us; but soul and heart formed a sublime essence in us long before our thoughts. The function of thought is to organize and arrange, and this is a good function and necessary for our social lives, but it has no place in the life of the heart and soul. 'If we should quarrel hereafter we must not go our separate ways'. Thought can say this despite being the cause of all quarrelling, but it cannot utter one word about love, nor is it able to measure the soul in terms of words, nor to weigh the heart in the scales of logic. (Gibran's *Little Book of Love* by Suheil Bushrui).

The above debate between the head and the heart does not mean we should stop using our brain when it comes to building relationships. What we are saying is that in addition to using our remarkable brain, we should learn more about using the untapped power of our heart to build great relationships. A loving, feeling and emphatic heart opens your narrow, biased mind to wider and clear consciousness, which brings the head and heart in perfect harmony for living a full life. "Western civilizations these days place great importance on filling the human 'brain' with knowledge, but no one seems to care filling the human 'heart' with compassion..... Cultivating a close, warmhearted feeling for others automatically puts the mind at ease. It helps remove whatever fears or insecurities we may have and give us the strength to cope with any obstacles we encounter," says Dalai Lama.

In fact, in our quest for building great relationships, we must honour our three-dimensional reality - body, mind and heart instead of focusing on a single dimensional way of life - the mind. This brings us to the concept of the relationship triangle as explained below:

Relationship Triangle

The quality and life of our relationships require that we learn to constructively balance our thoughts, emotions and passions – the three forces driving all relationships. Creating this balance, indeed, is the secret of building great relationships.

Do you know what a fire triangle is? Fire-fighters use this term to explain the mechanics of fire. Each side of the fire triangle represents an element of fire - fuel, air and spark (heat, energy). When all the three elements are present in appropriate proportions, a fire is bound to occur. Extending this analogy of fire to relationships, we propose a theory of the 'relationship triangle'.

The three sides of the relationship triangle are represented by love, passion, and commitment. On one side of the relationship triangle we have 'love', which is the feeling or emotion that originates from the heart. This is the spark or energy in the relationship triangle.

On the second side of the relationship triangle is 'passion', which are the sensual impulses, attraction, and thrill that connects one another. This is primarily a neurochemical phenomena connected with the physical body.

The third side of the relationship triangle is represented by 'commitment', which is the rational decision to stay in a relationship on a long-term basis. This is primarily the function of the brain.

When all the three components of a relationship – passion, commitment and love are present in right proportions, a great relationship will occur. Like in a fire, to keep the flame of a relationship alive, it is necessary to maintain these three components in proper proportions all the times.

There is, however, a difference between the fire and a relationship triangle. Unlike the fire triangle in which all the three sides are equal, the relationship triangle is a right-angled triangle with 'love' as its largest side, the hypotenuse. That shows we need love in higher proportion than passion or commitment, the other two components in relationships. Further in case of a fire, spark is needed to start it. Once started, it keeps going provided constant supplies of fuel and air are available. But to keep the flame of a relationship going, we need to provide the spark of love continuously, otherwise it would extinguish and the relationship will wither away. .

This concept of relationship triangle can be constructively used to build great relationships, only we need to combine the best the brain has created, and will create, with the wisdom of the heart, and vitality of our body. How to do that is the focus of the next chapter.

2

Nurturing Relationships

*The less you open your heart to others,
the more your heart suffers.*

Deepak Chopra

In the previous chapter, we learnt the theory of relationships.

For creating great relationships, we need to focus on our three-dimensional personality - body, mind and heart instead of working only with the mind as most of us do. We also learnt how our loving-heart plays the most crucial part in the relationship triangle. We will see the increasing role of our heart in the prescriptions for building different relationships – self, husband and wife, parents and children, and friends and coworkers, in the succeeding chapters of the book.

Our heart is the source of love that connects us to others. To live in great relationships we must learn and practise to contact our heart, open it; make it loving, compassionate and wholehearted. We call that as living from the heart. How to live from the heart? Since our heart is the seat of soul or spirit, we need to look for spiritual means to live from the heart. Contacting your own heart and connecting it to other hearts requires spiritual efforts. All love is based on the search for spirit.

Spiritual efforts! 'Heartless people' – non-believers and those with highly 'gifted' brains may doubt, even ridicule the efficacy of spiritual methods in our life and relationships. What perhaps, they do not know is that many modern day psychologists, scientists and doctors are coming up with theories and research that corroborates the power and wisdom of spiritual methods in our life and relationships. Experience shows that the psychological and family therapy approaches taught in most personal growth and relationship building seminars and books are of limited use when it comes to working with your heart or soul. The heart is better dealt with the spiritual methods than anything else.

Living by Heart

The prescriptions for nurturing great relationships given in this book are based on the practices of prayer, meditation, yoga, visualisation, rituals and others. These practices awaken the voice of our heart and cultivate love, compassion, gratitude and empathy; relax and broaden our minds and vitalise our body, all the virtues required to create great relationships.

These practices are drawn from time-tested wisdom of ancient scriptures and traditions of major world faiths, which are as relevant today as they were thousands of years ago. They are eternal and like the weight that holds a mason's plumb line straight and true, these spiritual principles never change, no matter what the circumstances. In most ancient and wise cultures, these virtues and their importance in our lives and relationships have been taught since time immemorial through rituals, stories, meditative skills and other spiritual traditions.

Unfortunately, at this point in history, our materialistic worldview, greed for more, individualistic culture and hurried lifestyle has made us selfish, hardened our hearts, corrupted our morality and changed our value system. Spiritual values, which used to be held as living principals by our forbearers find no place in our modern lifestyle, driven primarily by a heartless, compulsive mind. The result is disconnection, violence, depression, failed and often abusive relationships, sexual harassment and environmental neglect. It is time we go back and learn rather relearn our time-honoured spiritual methods to live a complete life in the vast human family here on this earth. The greatest need of the world today, we believe, is to embrace spiritual means.

In the following sections, we briefly introduce you to some of these wonderful, time-proven, spiritual processes, which form the basis of our suggestions made throughout this book on how to build great relationships. The beauty of these easy, yet radically transforming practices is that these invite you to step back from the rush and madness of the modern-day life, and take you to a realm of a relaxed body, a tranquil mind and a loving heart. As one practice cannot suit everyone, various methods have been suggested here, and everyone, by actual experience will find out what helps him most.

Prayer

The idea of prayer in one or the other form is very common in most cultures and traditions of the world. It is the most simple yet a powerful means to contact God and His creation. By prayer you are asking for the relationship, and also becoming the person worthy of that. When we pray, we surrender ourselves to the will of God. In surrender, our ego and pride, the biggest hurdles in relationships melt away. Ego and pride, which are the products of our intellectual minds, make us arrogant and insensitive to the feelings of others. Arrogance cuts us off from others. Humility, on the other hand, makes us teachable and reachable, which is particularly important in an intimate relationship.

It is necessary to get rid of arrogance and be humble in our dealings with others. We should be able to see beyond our limited ego or separate self. Prayer makes us humble, deepens insight, increases intuitive perception, expands consciousness, and transforms our personality. Prayer helps us discover ourselves. Through the act of prayer, you become more graceful, radiant, loving and magnetic.

In some cultures like Hinduism and Buddhism, new monks and *sadhus* are required to go through a practice of begging for food. It is not that they are poor or can't afford food, but it is a part of their training to control ego and inculcate humility. We are not suggesting you to go for begging like the monks do, but controlling ego and vanity is an important step to improve relationships, and prayer offers a very powerful way to do that.

Again, prayer is not a wishful thinking or a weak plea for something we are unable to do ourselves. It is, in fact, acknowledging God's generosity and greatness, and seeking blessing from Him in our genuine efforts to accomplish our task successfully. With prayer you focus on something specific, a defined purpose, and invite the divine power into your being to grace and strengthen you in your endeavour. That is why Francis Cardinal Spellman said, "Pray as if everything depended on God, and work as if everything depended upon man." A Sanskrit proverb – Prayer does not change God, but it changes him who prays.

Prayer is also a way to express our thanks and gratitude to God for the gifts of life: sunshine, water, food, and other things we need, and all our loved ones – father, mother, husband, wife, children, relatives and friends - who make our life meaningful. Gratitude is one of the greatest positive emotions, because it creates magnetism. A magnet draws things to itself, and therefore, giving heartfelt thanks for all the good around us makes us attract more good into our daily lives. When, in prayer, we say thank you God, we open our eyes to all the miracles around us.

Those who don't believe in the power of prayer may be inspired by APJ Abdul Kalam, former president of India who says, "I have been given everything I wanted in life – and much more. I don't feel the need to pray for myself. I pray for the nation, for the people of India, for the young minds that will take this country to the greatest heights." By praying not to get more, but to be more, we find a way to serve a purpose for which to live, and a dream to make real.

Let me share with you a small story on the power of prayer:

In a small town, a person decided to open up his bar business, which was right opposite a temple. The temple and its congregation started a campaign to block the bar from opening with petitions and prayed daily against his business. Work progressed. However, when it was almost complete and was about to open a few days later, a strong lightning struck the bar and it was burnt to the ground.

The temple folks were rather smug in their outlook after that, till the bar owner sued the temple authorities on the grounds that the temple through its congregation and prayers was ultimately responsible for the demise of his bar shop, either through direct or indirect actions or means.

In its reply to the court, the temple vehemently denied all responsibility or any connection that their prayers were reasons for the bar shop's demise.

As the case made its way into court, the judge looked over the paperwork at the hearing and commented: 'I don't know how I'm going to decide this case, but it appears from the paperwork, we have a bar owner who believes in the power of prayer and we have an entire temple and its devotees that doesn't.'

It is our firm conviction that God answers our prayers done with absolute trust and devotion. "The breeze of grace is always blowing on you. You have to open the sails and your boat will move forward," said Ramakrishna. In your prayer, you must have a keen desire for something. God fulfills your sanguine desires and does not provide you anything that you don't desire. There is a verse in *Ram Charitmanas*, the great Indian epic, *"Jeyi ko jeyi par satye saneyu, sou tai miley na kachhu sandeyu."* That means if you truly love to have something, be that a person, object, profession, reward, honour or any thing, you would surely get it without any doubt. The important thing is to develop a deep longing for the need and faith in God.

Make the habit of doing a daily prayer. No one can be so busy that he cannot find five minutes from his 24-hour day for prayer. Martin Luther King wrote in the 15th century, "I have so much to do today, that I shall spend the first three hours in prayer." Here are a few guidelines for praying.

- Sit in a comfortable position on the carpet or a chair. If you prefer to sit on the chair, your feet must rest firmly on the floor. Select a silent, secluded room or corner where there is no distraction.
- Relax your body by taking two-three deep breaths.
- Gently close your eyes, mentally looking at the picture or idol of any deity that you believe in. If you don't believe in a deity, imagine the formless God.
- Surrender to God with folded hands, and make your request sincerely and longingly. Ask God to grant you a loving, caring and compassionate heart.
- You may sing some song in praise of God.
- Practise for 5-10 minutes or more.

There are numerous prayers in scriptures and daily prayer books that one can sing. Find what interests you. A beautiful prayer written and sung by Rabindranath Tagore goes like this:

This is my prayer to thee my lord;

Give me strength rightly to bear my joys and sorrows;

Give me the strength to make my love fruitful in service;

Give me the strength never to disown the poor or bend my knees before insolent might.

Give me the strength to raise my mind high above daily trifles.

And give me the strength to surrender my strength to thy will with love.

Silence and Solitude

"Silence is the language of God. Everything else is a broad translation," said Monk Father Thomas Keating. Modern high tech life, filled with cell phones, with fax and answering machines, with e-mail, and with 24x7 television that offers countless channels, is more chaotic than in the past. Each one of us must find his balance between the need to connect with others, and the need to connect with ourselves. Solitude puts one in touch with his or her deepest feelings, and brings balance and harmony in life. When we do not get enough solitude; we get out of touch with ourselves, we get forgetful and stressful. If we put it simply, all of humanity's problems arise from man's inability to sit quietly in a room alone.

Silence and solitude deepens our awareness of life. It gives birth to creativity. Silence cures all afflictions caused by stress and strain, tensions and troubles, anxiety and confusion. It strengthens our immune system. "Silence is the birthplace of happiness. It is where we get outbursts of inspiration, feelings of compassion, empathy and love. That's the silence we want to bring into our awareness through meditation," says Deepak Chopra, MD, the modern spiritual guru.

Regularly take time to be alone. Sit in silence and practise *Swadhaya,* which is self-study and analysis. Contemplate on questions: Who am I? Where I am going? What is my goal? How am I going to reach there? By self-reflection, recreate yourself. Don't misunderstand recreation as 'goofing off'. Instead, look at the word as 'Recreation'. In moments of silence, realise that you are recontacting your source of pure awareness? Pay attention to your inner life, so that you can be guided by intuition rather than externally imposed interpretations of what is or isn't good for you.

Mother Teresa said, "See how nature - trees, flowers, grass grows in silence; see the stars, the moon and the sun, how they move in silence. We need silence to be able to touch souls."

Meditation

Practically every spiritual and religious tradition includes some form of meditation which is a subtle technique of making your mind and heart peaceful. During school days we were taught how to focus sunrays through a lens. In the simple experiment most of us did, a lens was moved on a piece of paper till the brightest spot emerged on the paper. By holding the lens focused for a while, the intense heat energy produced by the concentrated sunrays burnt the paper. Meditation is like performing this experiment that enables us to focus on our scattered energies.

Regular meditation concentrates our diffused mental and emotional energies, thereby burning the negative tendencies that are barriers to our progress in life and relationships. During meditation you let go of thoughts, images, stories and opinions and discover that you are not separate from life itself. The separate in you dissolves and great love is free to flow in your relationship and life.

When you sit quiet in meditation, every cell in your body is awake, alert, and energized. You become clear in your mind and sensitive to your feelings. You see how the flame of emotions is fuelled and fanned by your thoughts, which arise in your mind. These thoughts gradually die down and lose their hold on your attention. Soon you feel your emotions arising from your heart filling your entire body with love, compassion and empathy for others that is most directly applicable to relationships.

Meditation makes us light-headed and warm-hearted that enables us to become mentally and emotionally less reactive, and less likely to get hurt by our relationship problems. By regularly practising meditation the walls of hatred, likes and dislikes that we build around us, come down, and new energy, vitality, and love flow in bringing the relationships back to life.

Besides making you light-headed and warm hearted, meditation results in many positive health benefits to the body, including slower breathing and heart rate, lowered blood pressure, and relaxation of tense muscles. While you sit in meditation, you also get to know any pains, cramps, stiffness and other limitations of the body that need attention.

Some people misunderstand meditation to be sitting ideally shirking one's work. As Thich Nhat Hanh, the noted philosopher from South Vietnam said, "Meditation is not to escape from society, but to come back to ourselves and see what is going on. Once there is seeing, there must be acting. With mindfulness, we know what to do and what not to do to help."

"Before embarking on important undertakings, sit quietly, calm your senses and thoughts, and meditate deeply. You will then be guided by the great creative power of spirit," said Sri Paramhansa Yogananda in his book, *The Law of Success*. Indeed, meditation has great power. It can transform a person radically. Allow me to share a personal account on how meditation can totally change one's outlook to life and relationships.

During my seven years assignment in a large petroleum refinery in the Caribbean during 1990s, I had a Spanish-speaking colleague, named David (name changed), who was very egoistic, arrogant and often running into problems with people at work. At times, he would have problems at home also. I used to advise him to pray and meditate regularly. Although he occasionally came to our yoga classes, but never showed any interest in meditation or prayer. Being a very close friend and colleague, I tried to help him, but he was never serious about changing his behaviour.

After completing my contract with the refinery I returned to India. For three-four years we were in touch through e-mail, but then he stopped writing to me. My e-mails were also bouncing back. I learnt from some other friend that David lost his job in 2002 when the company went downsizing, but I had no contact with him. It was a great surprise to receive an e-mail from David after a lapse of almost five years. What a changed man he was now! I reproduce his e-mail verbatim. Never mind his language, he is basically Spanish speaking.

Senior Trehan. We are ok. I am in peace with myself. The most important elements of my life are now better than ever. My family is excellent. We are more integrated; we are having more time to share with each other.

What occurred in 2002 has been an opportunity for us. There is another world which is normally forgotten when one is fully involved in professional duties. This world is inside us; it is not easy to be found, but when you just 'touch' it, then fears, anxiety, etc. becomes part of the past and our way of feeling, existence start being different. I am more patient, sure about my 'today', looking for a future without extreme effort. Now I appreciate much more the wonders of simple things that the natural world gives to me. We spend so much time looking for the wrong fortune, having the right one in our own 'I'. After meditation, I realised about the inner power, the rest comes easy.

I am working for a petroleum company in Maracaibo, close to my family. Good salary, excellent work environment, good opportunity to help young co-workers, adding value. The ways of God are not so easy to understand, but at the end of the road we thank him, because we fall into account that is the most wonderful choice.

Gracias.

Did you notice how David got totally transformed through the magical power of meditation? He was now a very happy, relaxed and humble person, loving husband and an understanding boss. He is in regular touch with me through e-mails and often exchanges his insights on life and relationships. He was very happy when he learnt that I was writing a book on relationships.

There are many forms of meditation practised in different traditions, which can be grouped into two broad categories. One category that includes practices like mindful-breathing, imagery, visualization, relaxation response, and positive affirmation, etc. are basically mind-based techniques, which induce an altered state of focused attention and heightened awareness.

The other category of meditation is mainly the heart centre meditation, which is essentially an emotional-based technique to open and expand one's heart. In heart meditation, we become aware of our emotions instead of mental reflections. Here we focus on the heart in the centre of the chest cavity. This place, called the heart centre or *Anahata Chakra* in the yogic terminology, is dedicated to love, overcoming of separation and isolation. When this centre or *chakra is* blocked, we feel a sense of alienation from others. Concentrating on the heart centre, we experience the past feelings of love, caring, and appreciation stored there. It is a very useful practice to open, expand your loving heart and make it wholehearted. The essentials of heart meditation are explained briefly as under:

- Sit in a comfortable posture. Keep your back, neck and head in vertical alignment. If you have difficulty sitting on the floor, you may sit on a chair. In that case your feet should rest on the floor. You may place your hands on the knees.
- Close the eyes gently, and breathe slowly and deeply.
- Relax your body from head to feet.

- Bring your attention on the heart. Feel the palpitations of your heart and listen to the heartbeats.
- Focus your attention at the centre of the chest cavity. Imagine the flashes of deep blue colour emanating from the heart. Feel your heart expanding. Imagine the whole cosmos encompassed in your heart.
- Feel the expanse of the cosmos reducing to a tiny blue spot at the centre of the chest cavity. This is your soul or spirit residing in you.
- Continue for as long as you feel interested.

Following precautions will help you make your meditation better:

- Practise at least once a day for ten to twenty minutes or more. Remember that practice is necessary to progress at any thing.
- It is common to fall asleep or at least become drowsy when we first learn to meditate. The way to avoid this is to keep a straight back and not get too comfortable.
- Choose a quiet spot where you will not be disturbed by other people or by the telephone. Set aside a special place in your home for meditation.
- Set a fixed time for meditation. This may be morning, afternoon, evening or just before going to bed that suits your general schedule of work and other preoccupations.

Yoga

Yoga is the science and art of uniting with one's own self and with others. It brings the union of our mind, body and heart or the spirit to make us wholesome. Being wholesome, we experience a new vitality, feeling and clarity that affect our relationships at home, work and elsewhere. When properly practised, yoga offers help and insight into our relationship including our responsibility in them.

Successful relationships are built by respecting others and by paying proper attention to the people around us. Yoga increases your awareness and control, both physically and emotionally. It gives you peace of mind and freedom from fear. You start to feel a sense of ease with life, and you feel more able to adopt to change and accept other's viewpoints. Yoga makes the body strong yet flexible, alert yet relaxed and emotionally strong yet soft. With yoga, we begin to lead a life that is governed as much by the dictate of the heart and guts as by the rationale of the mind.

The traditional yoga, often called *Ashtangayoga*, the eight limbed yoga, comprises of *yama*, the code of conduct in society; *niyama*, self-discipline; *asana*, postures; *pranayama*, breath control; *pratayara*, contemplation; *dharana*, concentration; *dhyana*, meditation; and *samadhi*, super-consciousness.

Yama and *niyama*, the first two limbs of yoga help us develop healthy emotions that make us behave in a positive manner with our own selves, family, friends, and others in different situations. The five *yama* include: *Ahimsa*, non-violence; *Brahamcharya*, celibacy; *Satya*, truth; *Asteya*, non-stealing and *Aparigaya*, non-hoarding. The five *niyama* are: *Shaucha*, cleanliness; *Santosha,* contentment; *Tapas*, austerities; *Swadaya*, self-study and *Ishwarpranidhana*, dedication to God. Taken together, these are the ten yogic ethics of self-discipline that make us emotionally strong and creative. Without them life would be dull and we would function as machines, devoid of all feelings.

Asana, the third limb of traditional yoga is a technique, which places the physical body in certain positions, which stretch, twist or massage the body, thereby cultivating awareness, relaxation, and concentration. Certain specific body positions control hormonal secretions, and open energy channels, and psychic centers. All this helps to develop a healthy, young and vibrant physical body, a calm, peaceful and open mind, loving feelings and positive attitudes. "Asana penetrate deep into each layer of the body and ultimately into the consciousness," says BKS Iyengar, the yoga guru.

Pranayama, the fourth step of yoga is the science of correct breathing. The practice of *pranayama* makes us aware of our breathing. Various techniques of *pranayama* activate and regulate the vital life force that drives our life. Our breath becomes slow, deep and rhythmic, which allows oxygen to reach the remotest cell in the body, and expel toxins therein. This enhances the activity of each and every cell. *Pranayama* nourishes our whole body, gives us strength, dynamism, vigour and increases the life span.

The other four practices commonly referred as mediation are *pratyahara*, contemplation; *dharana,* concentration; *dhyana*, meditation; and *samadhi*, superconsciousness. All these practices are internal processes, which try to control the mind by fixing it to a central point of attention. These processes are very similar to each other, differing only in the intensity, duration or degree. We have already discussed meditation earlier in this chapter.

Robust health, a light body, a relaxed mind, freedom from cravings, always peaceful and poised, contented, unselfish, loving, friendly and ready to help others: these are some benefits you would get by practicing yoga regularly. Besides these benefits, yoga also enriches your sexual life, which is very important for a successful marital relationship, as we will learn in chapter 4. Asana, *pranayama* and meditation are the new ways to better sexuality.

Make a habit of practising asana and *pranayama* regularly for thirty minutes to one hour every day. Some simple yet very useful yogic practices include: Suryanamaskarasana, Pawanmuktasana, Bhujangasana, Ardhmatsyendrasana, Halasana, Sarvangasana, Siddhasana, Gorakhasana, Shashankasana, Ashwani Mudra, Moolbandha, Bhastrica Pranayama, Ujjai Pranayama, Anuloma-viloma pranayam. Our best selling book, *Effective Yoga – for Health and Happiness*, published by Macmillan Publishers India Ltd. can be a useful guide for learning various yogic practices.

Deep Mindful Breathing

The demands of the present-day competitive and tumultuous lifestyle bog you down. This is quite likely to have ill effects on your life and relationships. Relaxing your overworked body and mind is the first step towards a great relationship.

Deep slow breathing is the most simple yet very beneficial *pranayama* practice for relaxing the body and mind. It offers even the busiest people a precious opportunity to relax. This *pranayama* practice involves deep, slow and rhythmic breathing from your belly. That is how nature designed our respiratory system, so that we could assimilate maximum amount of *pranic* energy. But alas! Most people are shallow or short breathers. We all breathed properly when we were small kids. As we grow, we forget natural, deep and rhythmic breathing due to wear and tear of everyday stress, bad habits, and poor postures. We are always in a haste and do not have time even to breathe properly.

A deep and rhythmic breathing helps in removing various toxins in the body. When we inhale, the air is sucked in the lungs for gaseous exchange with the blood. During exhaling the waste gases from the blood are forced out of the body. When the breathing is short and shallow, the waste or stale air is not able to get out of the lungs, especially the lower extremities. Gradually, the toxins build up, and clog a large part of the lungs leading to a variety of respiratory disorders, fatigue and stress.

Deep, slow breathing has a calming effect on mind, reduces jumpiness, nervous tension, and increases our life span. A slow, deep breathing also increases the absorption of *pranic* energy enhancing vigour, vitality and general

well-being. The practice of mindful, deep breathing is briefly explained as under:
- Sit in a comfortable posture. Keep your back, neck and head in a straight line. You can do this practice lying in *Shavasana* also.
- Gently close your eyes. Taking a few normal breaths, relax your body.
- Keep your attention on the navel. Inhale deeply from the abdomen. The abdomen will bulge out when filled with air.
- Take a little pause for a fraction of a second and inhale more, now from the middle of the lungs expanding the ribs. The attention should shift to ribs.
- Again, take a little pause for a fraction of a second and inhale more, now from the top of the lungs, raising your shoulders. Your attention should now shift to the shoulders.
- In this way, you have taken the complete breath. The whole process should be like the links in a chain each merging into the next without any break. There should be no jerks or unnecessary strain. The breathing should be like the swell of sea.
- Hold the breath for a few moments.
- Now start exhaling slowly, first relaxing the upper chest, then the ribs, and finally the abdomen. Without straining, try to empty the lungs as much as possible by pulling the abdominal wall as near to the spine as possible.

The above constitutes one round. Practise ten to fifteen or more such rounds.

Yoganidra

Yoganidra or step-wise relaxation is another very effective way of relaxation. *Yoganidra,* also called progressive relaxation, is an internal tour or inspection of the body in which we pay attention to the various parts of the body one by one. When we pay attention to any part of the body, an increased supply of blood gets diverted from other parts of the body to irrigate that part abundantly, thereby relaxing and rejuvenating it.

The practice is best done in a comfortable lying position. However, if it is not feasible to lie down, you can do it while sitting on a chair. Here we describe the practice of *yoganidra* being done while lying down.

- Lie down on your back on a carpet or a bed, which is not too soft or too hard. Close your eyes gently and take two to three deep breaths.
- We generally start from the feet. Bring your attention to the toes of both the feet. Breathing slowly and easily, feel your toes as fully as you can. Imagine the toes going loose and relaxed. As the breath goes in and out, consciously let go of any tension in the toes.
- Then gradually shift your attention to ankles, calf muscles, knees, thighs, ribs, shoulders arms and hands. At each of these parts, hold the attention for a few seconds, let go of any tension and feel that part getting loose and relaxed.
- Then start from the genitals, and gradually move the attention to the abdomen, chest, neck, face, and head and to the back along the spine till the tailbone. At each of these parts, hold the attention for a few seconds, let go of any tension and feel that part getting loose and relaxed.
- You can even divide the body into still smaller parts and take each side of the body separately. For example, start with the right side – toes one by one, sole, heel, ankle, calf, knee, thigh, right half of abdomen, right rib cage, shoulder, upper arm, elbow, lower arm, wrist, palm, all the fingers one by one and then returning back to the right toes. Then repeat on the left side in the same way. After that take the tour of the middle of the

body starting from your genitals and going upward to the head and then to the back till the tailbone.
- Hold the attention on each part of the body for as much time as you have with you. Longer the time, the deeper and profound you relax.

In this way, the whole body gets loose, relaxed and rejuvenated. If you are slow, systematic and careful of your breath, you will be amazed, how deeply relaxed you can get. At the end of the practice, gently massage your eyes a few times with the roots of the palms. Open the eyes slowly and turning on the left side, get up in the sitting position. A twenty minutes to half-an-hour of *yoganidra* can be very relaxing and rejuvenating.

Rituals and Traditions

Rituals and traditions play an important role in promoting relationships. It is unfortunate that people these days devalue rituals and traditions as nonsense having no value to the present. These are things, which bind and bond us together. Observing rituals does not mean following blindly some old traditions and customs.

Social, cultural and religious festivals, group prayers, family meals, mass chanting and other similar occasions give us opportunities to come closer to others, and share our joy and grief with them. Going to church, temple, mosque or any other religious place is not only to worship God, who is present everywhere, and for that reason we need not go there, but also to congregate with like-minded people for *satsanga* or good company. "The whole purpose of religion is to facilitate love, compassion, tolerance, humanity and forgiveness," says Dalai Lama.

'Family meals' is a sacred ritual. Taking at least a meal together with all the members of the family could be a wonderful way to instil your love and values back into the family. Make it a regular part of your dinner routine. Thank God for bringing you together on the dinner table and the wonderful food on your plate. Similarly celebrate birthdays, wedding anniversaries, festivals, holidays, happy times, sad times, anything, which brings family together. These are all rituals and traditions that have kept many a family intact. They are no nonsense and blind faiths.

Praying together in the family or community is another ritual that promotes togetherness. "The family who prays together stays together," is a Christian advice. Group chanting of devotional songs and *kirtan* by members of ISKCON and Chaitanya Mahaprabhu sects have brought people and communities together and spread the gospel of universal brotherhood.

Charity is a great ritual to follow. It is same as generosity, giving or *daan* as in Sanskrit. You make a living by what you get, but you make a life by what you give. Giving provides a wonderful feeling of happiness and satisfaction. "Giving is the secret of a healthy life. Not necessarily money, but whatever a person has of encouragement, sympathy and understanding," said John D. Rockefeller Sr. There are numerous ways in which you can help others. "If you have much, give of your wealth; if you have little, give of your heart," says an Arabian proverb.

Help others, especially the poor and downtrodden by whatever means you can. Give your money, time, and energy to help others. Listen to them with regards. Care for others and think of their welfare. Do things for reasons other than furthering your own interests.

In the perspective of relationships, being charitable means giving of your love, affection, altruism, and intimacy to your loved ones unconditionally. "It is possible to give without loving, but it is impossible to love without giving," said someone. You live in vain if you do not have a generous heart. If you can remove selfishness and give love to others, half your relationship problems are over. Through selfishness you create a boundary wall around your loved ones.

The more you give, the more you will get. In fact, giving is a great virtue. *'Parhit bus jin ke manmahi, tin keq jag durlab kachhu nahi'* is a beautiful verse in Tulsi Ramayan (Aranyakand, 30.4) that highlights the virtue of benevolence. It says that nothing is impossible in this world for those who are generous and caring for the welfare of others.

When you give in charity, don't think you are a better person, rich, powerful, resourceful than the person you are giving. The true spirit of charity is giving, knowing that nothing, no attachment is ours to claim in the first place. Instead we are merely vessels through which universal abundance flows. We are the carriers of God who is the real giver. As Mother Teresa said, "Make us worthy, Lord, to serve those people throughout the world who live and die in poverty and hunger. Give them through our hands, this day, their daily bread, and by our understanding love, give them peace and joy."

Every act of giving is simultaneously an act of receiving. Each time you give something to someone, you are bound to receive even more than you have given. "Just as a healthy physical heart receives blood from the periphery which it then oxygenates and pumps back out, your emotional heart stays healthy by receiving and giving love in all its forms," says Deepak Chopra.

Building Great Relationships

How to create great relationships based on the concepts and practices learnt so far will be our focus in the next seven chapters to follow. Each of these chapters deals with a particular relationship. One chapter each has been devoted to the following relationships with which we interact more in our day-to-day life:

Self:	Chapter #3	Relating to your own self
Spouse:	Chapter #4	Marrying forever
Children:	Chapter #5	Art of parenting

Parents:	Chapter #6	Dealing with parents
Friends:	Chapter #7	Friends are treasure to keep
Coworkers:	Chapter #8	Workplace relationships
God:	Chapter #9	Relationship with God

The various prescriptions of healthy relationships given in the above chapters is all about understanding how to balance our emotions, passions, and commitments, the basic concept of the relationship triangle we discussed in the previous chapter. While you go through the various chapters of the book, you may refer back to the practices given here in this chapter as often as you require to ground yourself in them.

If, after reading the whole book, you find no improvement in your relationships, don't lose heart. Remember, this is an action book; mere reading will not help, you need to practise the methods given here. There is a yoga saying, "To experience is to live. To explain is to lie." Lasting relationships don't just happen; they are created. In the words of Swami Shivananda, "An ounce of practice is better than a ton of theory." Practice, practice, practice, for there is no other way to make it work. As someone said, "Before you've practiced, the theory is useless. After you've practiced, the theory is obvious."

3

Relating to Your Own Self

> Before we can have a successful relationship with anyone,
> we first need a perfect personal relationship.
>
> *- Russ Von Hoelscher*

The most important relationship to create is the one with your own self. Creating great relationships starts from you. Without starting there, you can't relate effectively to others. Who we are to ourselves determines who we are to others. It's impossible to be happy with your wife, husband, parents, children, friends, fellow-workers and others if deep inside you are not happy and peaceful with yourself. An individual who is at peace with himself is at peace with the whole world.

A deeper understanding of life and the ability to love and believe in the self is the greatest gift you can have. Make yourself worthy of this gift. "As human beings our greatness lies not so much in being able to remake the world as in being able to remake ourselves," said Mahatma Gandhi.

Since creating relationship with your own self is so important, we decided to begin with you before handling any other relationship. Before rushing into any kind of relationship, know yourself, feel yourself, respect and love yourself. By honouring yourself and treating yourself with respect, you create the environment for others to treat you with respect. To be happier with yourself and in your relationships, your first job should be to prioritise and bring order to your own life. How would you do that?

Know Thyself

Knowing yourself is a prerequisite for healthy and long-term relationships with others. Before you judge and criticise anyone else's defects, look inside who you are. I am a man, I am a woman, I am young, I am old, I am white skin, I am dark skin, I am tall, I am short, I am American, I am Indian, I am rich, I am poor. All these are only external tags by which most of us generally identify ourselves. We remain ignorant of our inner identity, our true self. Having a well-developed sense of self is a key aspect of being psychologically healthy and balanced. Many people, unfortunately, don't have a well-developed sense of self, which contributes greatly to relationship problems and alienation from one another.

Therefore, know your true self. Foremost, you must firmly believe that you are not a lonely soul in this world. Instead, you are part of the Whole, the bigger Self, or the all-pervading *brahm*, the Godhead. This concept of who you are is depicted as *Ahom Bramasi*, (I am God) in the *advaita* Hindu philosophy. The Vedic concept of *vasudev katubkam*, upholds that each one of us is a part of this great family of God on this earth. Many other cultures also believe that we are all children of God, who is our universal father.

Affirming yourself as part of God gives you the strength to be confident about yourself. You may be alone, but there is no reason to feel lonely. An intimate relationship with God can help diminish your loneliness. The reason you don't feel completely loved and lovable is that you don't identify with your true self, your spiritual self. Believe in God and that he is omnipresent, omnipotent and omniscient, nothing can go wrong.

In our day-to-day life we become so busy and absorbed that most of us forget who we are. When you sit in silence and contemplate (*swadhay*) on a regular basis, you get to know yourself better. In that silence, you notice things you never noticed before. You observe how busy your mind is, full of thoughts, judgements, plans and strategies. With regular practice, the mental chatter settles down and you start noticing patterns that reveal something about yourself. Our behavioural patterns are one of the primary reasons of our failures in relationships. These patterns are developed throughout our lifetime right from childhood to adolescence to adulthood till death. However, our preoccupation with mundane things of everyday life makes us ignorant of these patterns. Practice of *swadhay* helps to realise our shortcomings and provide us opportunity to correct them.

Love Yourself

Bible says, "Love your neighbour as yourself." Perhaps, one of the reasons we love our neighbours so poorly is that we never learnt how to love ourselves. You can't love others if you don't love yourself. As part of God, you are the mirror of divine beauty. Looking into the mirror, Rumi, the famous Sufi saint said:

> By God, when you see your beauty,
> You will be the idol of yourself.

Love yourself as you are. Appreciate and praise yourself the way you are, and avoid self-pity. Look into the mirror regularly and say aloud and confidently: "I am gorgeous, attractive and magnificent being, inside and out, head to toe. I love you, I really love you." Beware of your posture, walk tall with pride and confidence for who you really are, and move with grace. This is looking the mirror externally. Occasionally, also look into your heart's mirror with eyes closed. You will discover much more of you to be loved.

Always maintain a high degree of self-esteem. Self-esteem is how we see ourselves and how we think others see us. Do you love yourself the way you are? Do you have a friendly smile? Are you a great singer? Are you a great artist? Are you a great lover? Are you a loving parent? Are you proud of being a good friend? Reminding yourself of these positive qualities can help you feel good about yourself. Often reward yourself for the good deeds you do. For instance, give a big treat to yourself, if you succeeded in losing those extra kilos, quitting smoking or some other bad habit. Celebrate passing an exam or test. Give yourself the simple pleasures of life, not waiting for some big things to happen. Many people have the habit of hating or condemning themselves with feelings of negativities like:

      I am not beautiful or handsome

      I am too fat

      I am too skinny

      I am not young

      I look old

      I am nothing

      I am inadequate

      I am out of shape

      I hate my dress

      I hate my figure

      I don't deserve to love or be loved

      I can't perform the way I used to

      People don't notice me ......and so on

Stop living life in self-pity and self-blame. You are not as bad as you think. Be gentle, kind and patient with yourself. Don't hate yourself for having negative thoughts, but gently change them. Consciously generate positive thoughts and feelings of self-love in place of old thoughts of inadequacy. Often associate with others with high esteem. That is called *satsang*, the company of good, wise people. It helps to enhance your esteem.

Acknowledge yourself frequently with positive impressions about yourself. Avoid comparing yourself with others, and stop being critical of yourself and others. Evaluate yourself by your own standards, not someone else's. Stop taking yourself so seriously all the times. Laugh at yourself and at life, but not others.

Take full responsibility for your life. Don't waste time grieving over past mistakes; instead learn from them. Take all criticism as positive for it leads to self-evaluation. You have always the option of rejecting it if it is not fair or not applicable. Invest money in yourself. Buy books, attend seminars, workshops and courses that develop your talents. Make a list of five things you love doing and do them frequently.

Self-care of Body

Only a healthy person can enjoy the love of his or her spouse, children and other relations and friends. You need a healthy body to make use of the wonderful things, God has provided for our enjoyment. An unhealthy and diseased person is a curse to himself and the society. No body, even one's close relatives and friends would like a sick person. He is a burden to his family, society and the nation.

The importance of health cannot be over emphasised. Good health, besides absence of disease, and disability, includes being active, vital, sexually potent, mentally alert, emotionally strong, and with a definite purpose in life. In fact, good health is a state of being in balance with our physical, mental and spiritual beings.

Your body is the temple, abode of God, and it is your duty to keep it clean and healthy. Though modern research tells us that much of our health depends on our genes; there is no reason to take health and wellness for granted. Good health does not come by itself, we have to nurture it and maintain it. "Health is not a commodity to be bargained for. It has to be earned through sweat," says BKS Iyengar, the yoga guru. So, take basic good care of your health to get and stay in shape: eat well, exercise, rest etc. Remember the loving affirmation of the poet Louise Hay who said:

> I love myself:
>
> Therefore, I take loving care of my body,
>
> I lovingly feed it nourishing foods and beverages,
>
> I lovingly groom it and dress it,
>
> And my body lovingly responds to
>
> me with vibrant health and energy.

Diet

Diet is a key factor of health and longevity. The phrase 'we are what we eat' is now supported by scientific research. A balanced diet of wholesome, nutritious, low-fat foods promotes health and well-being. Such a diet is abundant in plant foods like whole grains, beans, peas, lentils, vegetables, and fruits; low in fat (especially saturated fat) from meat, dairy products and oils; and with right amount of calorie to maintain a healthful weight. Adequate consumption of vitamins, minerals, and fiber collectively called as micro-nutrients is very essential especially for elderly people to help repair, maintain and restore worn out and damaged cells and tissues. A diet that supplies optimal amounts of vitamins and minerals helps a person not only avoid disease, but also feel his or her best with the emotional and physical health necessary to enjoy relationships and life to it's fullest.

The selection of food is a discipline, which requires careful thought, attention and choice. It is healthy to eat a wide variety of food to get optimal nutrition. Though eating vegetarian or non-vegetarian food is a matter of personal preference, tradition or availability, there is a growing awareness of the benefits of vegetarian diet worldwide. Besides reducing the chances of many degenerative diseases, vegetarian diet makes you cooler, more passionate and loving person. In *Ayurveda*, it is believed that the violence, cruelty and aggression suffered by the animals when they are slaughtered, appears in the form of increased level of anger, intolerance and other violent behaviour in people, who eat the meat of those animals. "Nothing will benefit human health and increase chances of survival of life on earth as much as the evolution to a vegetarian diet," said Albert Einstein.

Alcohol, smoking and drugs are not only harmful to your health they are also a cause of many relationship problems. These addictions have ruined many lives and relationships. It is better to avoid them. Alcohol in moderation is okay, but one has to find out one's limits.

Exercise

Physical activity and regular exercise are important for your health and well-being. A good exercise done regularly improves metabolism, boosts immune system, strengthens the heart, lowers high blood pressure, relieves stress, and helps in losing weight and in coping with host of other crippling diseases. Exercise increases blood circulation in our body, which helps to distribute the nutrients we take in through food to various cells of the body for their proper functioning. There are many exercises- swimming, cycling, gym workouts, treadmill, weight lifting, gymnastics, calisthenics, dancing, athletics, walking, jogging, running, yoga and other field supports. What exercise you should do depends on your personal choice, occupation, age, sex, body constitution and other conditions.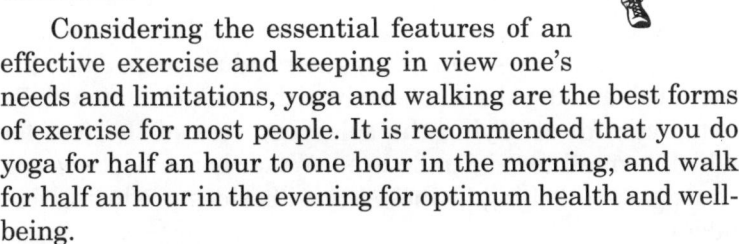

Considering the essential features of an effective exercise and keeping in view one's needs and limitations, yoga and walking are the best forms of exercise for most people. It is recommended that you do yoga for half an hour to one hour in the morning, and walk for half an hour in the evening for optimum health and well-being.

Personal Hygiene

Personal hygiene is not only important for disease-free good health; it is also a very important factor for good relationships. Foul smell from mouth, underarms, stinking socks, and other unpleasant odours from your body may be sufficient reasons for others, even your intimate close-ones to keep a distance from you. It is important that you take adequate care in keeping your body clean and pleasant looking. Most cultures in the world, equate cleanliness with virtue.

Our teeth tell a lot about us. Good dental care not only keeps teeth healthy and helps us to taste and assimilate food better; it also brings us closer to people. Make it a habit to brush your teeth at least twice a day – once in the morning before taking bath, and in the night before going to bed. If possible, use *neem datun* (a small stick of *neem*-tree made into a brush) to clean your teeth. *Neem* is excellent for protecting teeth from bacterial infections and foul smell from the mouth. It is true that the availability of *neem* is a problem in the modern urban living, but if we are serious we will find it.

Take a good bath every day with cold or hot water depending on the climate. Avoid excessive use of soap as it takes away body oils making the skin dry. Use a mild soap on those areas of the body, which are more prone to sweat like armpits, neck, under the knees, and the genitals. Wash off all the soap from the body thoroughly, with plenty of water. Any left over soap will create severe dermatitis. We have known many cases of acute skin problems, especially of the private parts, caused by the residual soap. After the bath, rub and dry the whole body with a soft, clean towel. Be extra careful of drying the soles and toes of the feet for which a small towel can be used. Water borne bacteria can cause severe itching in these areas, besides producing foul odour.

One should don a comfortable dress to protect oneself from vagaries of weather. Though the choice of dress will depend on climatic conditions, ethnic background, personal tastes, economic standards, and many other factors. Some basic points need to be given careful thought before you make a choice of your dress. The dress should not be too tight that restricts the movement of muscles, hampers proper breathing and perspiration. Avoid apparels made of synthetic materials, if possible. Lighter colours are preferred especially in hot climates. Use clean and loose undergarments - vest, bra, underwear, panties and others preferably made of cotton. Change the undergarments and socks everyday.

Many people have the habit of overlooking the simple facts of keeping their body clean, and try to camouflage bad body odours by overuse of deodorants and cosmetics, which can be harmful in the long run. There are no shortcuts to personal hygiene as explained above.

Where Are You Going?

Life today is very busy and fragmented. We are in hurry, in the fast lane and seem to be trying to fit more and more into the same fixed 24x7 schedule. It's not only the scenery you miss by going too fast you also miss the sense of where you are going and why. At the end of the day we get irritable and drained.

Stress and tension in your body, coupled with worry and hurry of the present times can be barriers to enjoy great relationships. When we overwork, when we rush from place to place, we lose track of what is important and in doing so we often sacrifice the values, which support our relationships. If we look patiently, we may wonder what it is all about. You may ask yourself if the sky will fall down, hell will break, someone will die, or the world will stop working if you sit down for five minutes to relax and feel peaceful.

Slow down and relax. The great writer HG Wells said, "Soul cannot exist when our connections in life remain superficial. An experience of soul requires that we take time to be fully present to the details of our lives. Explore what happens when you take time to stop and pay attention. When we choose to slow down and really experience the qualities of our lives, we get a whole new perspective on what living is all about."

However much we have to do, there is no need to be in hurry. There is no value in living crisis to crisis. Dwight Eisenhower said, "Truly important things are seldom urgent and urgent things are seldom truly important." Get your priorities straight. No one ever said on his deathbed, "Gee, if I'd only spent more time at the office."

A company executive was always in haste and stressful. One day he was rushing for a meeting and asked his secretary, "Miss Rita, I don't find my pencil? You are always careless and don't keep the things in order." "Sir," the frightened girl replied, "It is right behind your ear." "You know how busy I am! Which ear?" shouted the executive.

Are you really so busy or pretending to be? Both ways it can be very stressful. Stress is the basic cause of a host of ailments like depression, hypertension, heart diseases, sexual dysfunction, ulcers, diabetes, arthritis, etc. Stress is a silent killer, which spares nobody. If there is one thing that can shatter the hopes of a good relationship, it is stress. We must, therefore, learn to strike a balance between our work and family.

The Comedian Inside You

"Life is a mirror. If you frown at it, it frowns back; if you smile, it returns the greetings," said someone. A generous amount of laughter is essential to healthy, hopeful lifestyle, cures almost all of life's ills. It can quickly bring feelings of joy and connection. "A sense of humour is a part of  the art of leadership, of getting along with people, of getting things done," said Dwight D. Eisenhower.

Sigmund Freud said that laughter is a release of energy. I want to go a step further and say that laughter releases toxic gases, which if not released become increasingly combustible that may burn you and your relationships. Use laughter as a safety valve to keep yourself and others sane and relaxed.

'He who laughs, lasts long' and 'laughter, the best medicine', are age-old adages. Even scientific data indicates that a good, hearty laugh promotes secretion of endorphins, the chemicals that cause good feelings. Laughing can be a good exercise. When we laugh, our stomach and so many muscles of the face are exercised. "If I had no sense of humor, I would long ago have committed suicide," said Mahatma Gandhi.

A smile is an inexpensive way to improve your looks. Those who laugh whole heartily, also show more courage and confidence. Besides being healthy, a good smile promotes goodwill and service. In South Korea, for example, where smiling has traditionally been frowned upon, some people now consider laughter a business skill that is increasingly necessary, as customers demand better service.

Joy, humour, laughter are all wonderful, easily accessible tools for bringing comfort to a relationship. They can help you overcome inhibitions and tensions. Dr. Williams Fry of Stanford University has just recently reported that laughter aids digestion, stimulates the heart and strengthens muscles, and activates the brain's creative functions and keeps you alert. All this is possible with only just a hearty guffaw!

So, laugh wholeheartedly whenever you get a chance forgetting any feeling of shame or hesitation. You need not wait for a funny thing to happen to have a hearty laugh. You can start laughing any time, even right now. Put the book aside, and laugh loudly from the bottom of your tummy and feel its good effects.

No wonder most of us have a little comedian inside us who wants to express great humour, but we don't allow it to come out. It is a pity that the modern, civilised man considers laughing as bad social etiquette, and refrains from laughing even when his heart really wants to laugh. In many societies and cultures around the world, laughing loud is taken as bad manners. Then there are people who laugh at other's misery or suffering. This kind of laughter is resorted to by people who are overwhelmed by pride, hatred and jealousy, and is not healthy.

Interestingly, of late, people have started realising the importance of laughing. A number of 'laughing clubs' have sprung up in big cities where people share their hearty laughs in groups. That is a healthy trend. Become a member of such a club to let your little comedian come out.

Don't Worry What Others Say

Different people have different perceptions. One man's meat could be another man's poison. You can never have everyone praise you, nor will everyone condemn you. Do not be too bothered by other peoples' words, if your conscience is clear.

You must have heard the story of a couple that bought a donkey from the market. On the way home, a boy commented, "Very stupid! Neither of them ride on the donkey?" Upon hearing that, the husband let the wife ride on the donkey, and walked beside them. Later, an old man saw and commented, "The husband is the head of family. How can the wife ride on the donkey while the husband is on foot?" Hearing this, the wife quickly got down and let the husband ride on the donkey. Further on the way home, they met an old Lady. She commented, "How can the man ride on the donkey but let the wife walk. He is no gentleman." The husband thus quickly asked the wife to join him on the donkey. Then, they met an animal lover. He commented, "Poor donkey, how can you hold up the weight of two persons. They are cruel to you." Hearing that, the husband and wife immediately climbed down from the donkey and carried it on their shoulders. It seemed to be the only choice left. Later, on a narrow bridge, the donkey was frightened and struggled. The couple lost their balance and fell into the river along with the donkey.

The story of couple and the donkey may not be true, but it teaches us a great lesson. Do you notice how the couple ruined themselves by trying to satisfy everyone? Most of us do the same mistake by trying to please others. We are afraid what people will say if I did this thing, if I wore this dress, if I sat this way, if I ate this or that food and so on. Our whole life goes in worrying about how others see us. "I care not what others think of what I do but I care very much about what I think of what I do," said Theodore Roosevelt.

Again quite often, we say 'yes' to everyone to please or satisfy him or her, knowing very well we can't do what he or she are asking for. So, we need to learn to say 'no' if the situation demands. Being 'yes minister' all the times, does no good. One should not be afraid what people would say, if you said 'no'. There is no way we can agree with everyone and please them, and still be real, authentic people. In the end, nothing will create more stress and tension than trying to please everyone. "He who is afraid of people's censure, will never be able to do anything worthwhile," said Mahatma Gandhi.

Every day we come across people doing good things, people doing bad things, people we like, people we hate, and people who simply drive us mad. As long as we are in this world, this is unlikely to change. So, learning not to take every situation seriously is the right attitude. However, many people are oversensitive and get unnecessarily disturbed on small issues, adding to their own difficulties. The Dalai Lama said rightly, "We often add to our pain and suffering by being overly sensitive, overreacting to minor things, and sometimes taking things too personally. We tend to take small things too seriously and blow them out of proportion."

Don't Judge Others, Judge Yourself

Before we give any criticism, it might be a good idea to check our state of mind and ask ourselves if we are ready to see the good rather than to be looking for something in the person we are about to judge.

Once a young couple moved into a new neighbourhood. Next morning, while they were eating breakfast sitting in their apartment, the young wife saw her neighbour hang the washed clothes outside in the balcony for drying.

"That laundry is not very clean", the young wife said. "She does not know how to wash correctly. Perhaps she needs better laundry soap." Her husband looked on, but did not say anything.

Every time her neighbour would hang her clothes to dry, the young wife would make the same comments. About one month later, the young wife was surprised to see a nice clean wash on the line and said to her husband, "Look! She has learnt how to wash correctly. I wonder who taught her this."

The husband said, "I got up early this morning and cleaned our windows."

And this is the same in our lives: What we see when watching others depends on the purity of our mind's window through which we look. Many a times, our eyes deceive us. What our eyes see may not be true unless we know the background.

Tap Your Inner Resources

As a refinery manager I learnt how to manage efficiently the material resources, energy resources, financial resources and human resources in the oil and gas industry. And that is what most managers do. It is only when I started practising yoga in the later phase of my professional career that I realised the importance of what we call the 'inner resources' – faith, contentment, humility, generosity, honesty, service, perseverance and so on. Yes, these are the inner forces, which if tapped timely and sincerely, provide remarkable strength to our persona. What I learnt was that no matter how difficult our tasks and the challenges might be, whether at work, home, society or elsewhere, the incredible power of these human qualities helps us to handle them easily and gracefully.

Describing all these human qualities in detail would require a full volume. Because of space limitation we will briefly dwell on a few which are more fundamental and have great bearing on many others. Faith is one such quality. It is among the most powerful inner resource at your disposal, which can transform your whole life.

Faith

Webster partially defines faith as an unquestioning belief in God with complete trust, confidence, and reliance. When a father throws his two years child in the air, the child still smiles than being afraid of falling on floor because he believes that his father will catch him in his safe arms. This is faith.

Faith is not just waiting, hoping, and wanting things to happen. Rather it is working hard to make things happen, and realising that there are no failures, just disappointments, when you have done your best. Always think positive that whatever is happening is happening for our good. "Faith is taking the first step even when you don't see the whole staircase," said Martin Luther King, Jr.

Faith is a powerful engine that drives our lives. It makes us humble and frees us from arrogance. Former Indian president APJ Kalam says, "When I look up into the sky, I see a million stars. One star- the sun- is enough to keep our whole solar system running. We are yet to discover how many more solar systems are there. The thought is overwhelming! It makes me realise that we are just specks in the universe. It gives me reason to believe that there is something, somewhere that I can turn to. And so, I pray."

There are times in life when you may face difficult situations, and all your faculties seem inadequate. All avenues of help are closed. At such times keeping your faith will show you the way. "I have been driven many times to my knees by the overwhelming conviction that I had nowhere else to go. My own wisdom and that of all about me seemed insufficient for the day," said Abraham Lincoln.

Ronald Reagan has been one of the most eloquent of America's presidents. One day, Elizabeth Dole, his public liaison assistant asked him, "Mr. President, you have the weight of the whole world on your shoulders, yet you are always so kind and gracious. How do you do that?' He said, "Well, Elizabeth, when l was governor of California, each morning began with someone standing before my desk describing yet another disaster. The feeling of stress became almost unbearable. I had the urge to look over my shoulder for someone I could pass the problem to. One day I realised that I was looking in the wrong direction. I looked up instead of back. I'm still looking up, I couldn't face one more day in this office if I didn't know I could ask God's help and it would be given."

Contentment

Santosha or contentment is another very profound inner resource that has a great significance in our lives and relationships. *Santosha,* means to be happy with what you have. It is a key *niyama* in the yoga tradition that teaches you how to enjoy what you have, and to be able to lose all desire for things beyond your reach.

Contentment is a state of mind where we feel satisfied with what we have. A discontented mind always looks at what others have that he does not, and is therefore never at peace. The people who are contented are the happiest of all. Much of the stress in our lives is the result of our inability to be contented. The scriptures say that we must not get swayed away in the storm of materialism and consumerism, but must live a life of contentment in all situations. William Shakespeare wrote beautifully:

> My crown is in my heart, not in my head,
> Nor decked with diamonds and Indian stones,
> Nor to be seen; my crown is called contentment;
> A crown it is, that seldom kings enjoy.

Contentment does not mean that you don't put efforts to improve your present situation. As long as you look for reasonable, practical, and ethical ways of meeting your needs, it is fine, and you must strive for it to live a happy life. But, if you want fancy possessions, all the worldly pleasures, do whatever you like, buy a 15 million dollar lingerie, have a quarter million pounds dinner with friends like John Elton does, holidaying in space, and so on, there is no end to your miseries. If we want to live happily, we must separate out what we really need from the superficial things, we are chasing madly. How to enjoy what you have, and to control craving for things beyond your reach, is the secret of contentment.

Although, it is necessary to satisfy your core needs and desires in order to be fulfilled in life and relationships, you must be clear and articulate what you really want. We have a friend, called Mike David, who lives in our neighbourhood in Chicago. Mike, a fifty years old auto-salesman is very jovial. We saw him often in his front garden, watering the plants, during our evening walk. One day, after chatting with him for a while, I bade him good-bye saying "God bless you a happy and peaceful life." "But how can one be happy without money," he replied emphatically. "But you have a beautiful wife, a big house, two cars and all the other comforts of life," I added. "But that is not enough," he said. "Then how much money you want that will make you happy," I asked him jokingly. "May be a million dollars," he said curiously. I wished him good luck.

Now, if like Mike, you think a million dollars can buy you happiness, and you run madly to get it, you are utterly mistaken. There are plenty of millionaires, even billionaires in this world who are unhappy!

One thing we must understand, and that is, that money is not everything. The ultimate aim of every one in life, irrespective of what he or she is or what he or she does is to feel happy. David Navin, Ph.D. author of *The 100 Simple Secrets of Happy People* says, "Although people believe that as you get wealthier, you get happier, studies show that if you have enough money to feed and clothe yourself, more money does not increase happiness." Happiness depends to a significant degree on your expectations. If you inflate your expectations, you are just begging to be unhappy.

Contentment guards us against many emotional enemies like anger, greed and others that cause lot of harm in our life. Anger leads to all sorts of problems - problems at work, in your personal relationships, and in the overall quality of your life. Rage is the worst form of anger, which is uncontrolled and destructive. During a fit of rage, one loses control over one's nerves with resulting actions that may be regretted later. When you are angry, you burn yourself like a matchstick, which burns its own tip first before burning any other object.

Anger and greed have a common root. They spring from our cravings and inflated desires. Our inflated desire for sensorial objects produces craving for a particular thing. We try to get that thing by hook or by crook. If we get the object, we feel happy, which does not last long. Then there is a further desire for what we consider to be a better object. We try to get that too. This leads to a still bigger desire, we want to satisfy. This tendency results in greed, *lobha,* which breeds many other ills. On the other hand when the desired object is not obtained, there is frustration, anger, and we lose the mental balance. So, the key to control the negative emotions of anger, frustration and greed is to limit our desires, have contentment.

Sigmund Freud, the famous psychologist said, "When making a decision of minor importance I have always found advantageous to consider all pros and cons. In vital matters, however, such as the choice of a mate or a profession, the decision should come from the unconscious, from somewhere within our selves. In the important decision of personal life we should be governed, I think, by the deep inner needs of our nature."

Humility

Humility is a core inner strength that sustains our relationships. It is the opposite of ego, and you know how ego comes into the way of healthy relationships. Dr. A.B. Simpson, the famous Canadian theologian sums up humility in this way: "Humility will save you from self-consciousness. It will take away from you the shadow of yourself and the constant sense of your own importance. It will save you from self-assertion and from thrusting your own personality upon the thoughts and attention of others. It will save you from the desire for display, from being prominent, from occupying the centre of the stage, from being the object of observation and attention, and from having the eyes of the world upon you."

4

Marrying Forever

> Marriage resembles a pair of shears, so joined that they cannot be separated, often moving in opposite direction, yet always punishing any one who comes between them.
>
> *Sydney Smith, English writer*

We are born, live and grow in relationships with others. At one or the other point in our lives, most of us want to have a special relationship with a life partner, a very intimate lover and companion. This relationship is called marriage, which is the union of a man, the husband and a woman, the wife. Without marriage our lives will not be complete. It is only through marriage that Nature intended us to procreate and continue her cycle of creation.

Marriage is a sacred union of two loving and compassionate souls who commit to remain in partnership together throughout their lives. "What greater thing is there for two human souls than to feel that they are joined for life - to strengthen each other in all labour; to rest on each other in all sorrow, to minister to each other in all pain, to be one with each other in silent, unspeakable memories at the moment of last parting," said George Elliot, the English novelist.

And in Hindu philosophy, this union is not only for one lifetime but for seven lives, and it is for this reason that the relationship between husband and wife is called *saat janamo ka saath*. Most relationships inevitably change over time. For instance, your equation with your children will change as they grow up, with your friends and relatives as you become older, but you have in your spouse someone who will always be by your side, and with whom you can share your secrets, your moments of happiness and sorrow till the last moment.

Unfortunately the sacred and profound relationship of marriage has taken a lot of beating and abuse during the last couple of decades. Nowadays, marriages are increasingly ending in acrimony and divorce. In some western societies, nearly 50 per cent marriages end in divorce. Fascinated by multimillion dollars divorce judgements awarded by civil courts, couples in many countries are flooding the courts with divorce applications. In fact, the great institution of marriage has become the institution of misery for many. Why are there so many troubled marriages?

Troubled Marriages

In earlier times, the couples were contented and honoured their commitment to one another. They made space for each other, and worked together towards self-improvement by helping each other in times of distress. But today the couples split apart on small, insignificant issues, making marriage a mockery or a child's play. In a recent survey on married couples conducted in Britain, 56 per cent admitted they were not happy in their relationship – and more than half said that they had considered at some point of time splitting from their partner. Most of the wives surveyed said they would divorce immediately if their future economic security was assured.

Contrary to the concept of marriage as a lifetime relationship of love, commitment and security, it has become a matter of convenience. Marry today, break tomorrow, is becoming order of the day in many societies, especially the developed West. Why even marry, when you can have live-in relationships, which is legally accepted in many countries. Or have a causal sexual relationship with no ties or even be a single parent if you desire. These rampant alternatives to a legal, solemnized marriage are quite common in many developed, western societies.

Even in our culture where marriage has been held sacred, there is a growing tribe of youngsters living together out of wedlock. Read these excerpts from a report published recently in a national daily, on how some young people view relationships: "I just cannot get into a relationship with him. He's too laidback about love, relationships and responsibility. But I can't get over him either – the sex is so good. We've decided to keep our relationship primarily physical till either one of us finds someone special," says a young woman. "I think every guy would love to have a girl in his life who he can call, have sex with and not see again till he chooses to. But Indian girls have too many hang-ups and always claim to fall in love or become clingy," says a young man.

The sacred institution of marriage has lost its significance in the present-day world consumed by materialism, comfort and convenience. A few decades ago, live-in relationships were viewed with awe. How dare a couple cohabit without being legally bonded in matrimony? But things have changed a lot. Today, many people live out of wedlock for convenience, freedom and thrill. They say marriage involves additional responsibility and commitment, and therefore not necessary. Salman Rushdie, controversial Indian-origin author of *The Satanic Verses*, said in a recent interview for the Elle magazine, "It's strange, given that I've been married four times, but I actually don't think marriage is necessary." It is really strange that Salman, a veteran of four marriages and an equal number of divorces feels marriage is not necessary.

Have you read in the news recently how some vested interests in the western world are abusing the sacred institution of marriage by promoting divorce under the guise of helping troubled marriages? A new magazine, *Rosenkrieg* is being published in a small town near Munich, Germany since 2006 that exclusively deals with divorce. The objective of this bimonthly magazine is to facilitate its readers, how to achieve perfect dissolution of marriage. Strange! Isn't it? Instead of helping how to build strong relationships and repair broken marriages, the magazine facilitates its readers how to get an instant divorce, and get maximum benefits out of it.

And Vienna, Austria hosted the World's first divorce fair in October 2007, which attracted a large number of couples with troubled marriages, exhibitors, lawyers, financial advisors, mediators, private detectives and DNA laboratories. The fair offered a whole lot of services on rights and obligations of prospective divorcees, alimony, child access, paternity test, and how best to organize their new post-married lives. The only thing the fair did not have was, any suggestions on how to reduce the number of marriage breakdowns. Well, that is our focus in this chapter.

Finding a Perfect Partner

A man visited a matrimonial agency and requested, "I am looking for a wife. Can you please help me to find a suitable one?" The agent asked for his requirements. "Oh, good looking, polite, humorous, sporty, and knowledgeable. She should be good in singing and dancing. Willing to accompany me the whole day at home during my leisure hour when I don't go out. Telling me interesting stories when I need a companion for conversation, and be silent when I want to rest." The agent listened carefully and replied, "I understand you need a television, not a wife."

Are you looking for a life partner or a television? First be practical, and don't skyrocket your expectations for an ideal or perfect partner. Don't look for a perfect partner, as no one is perfect. Instead look for the right partner. "God help the man who won't marry until he finds a perfect woman, and God help still more if he finds her," said Benjamin Tilleti. A successful marriage depends on two things: one finding the right person and second being the right person. Assuming you being the right person, how do you go finding the other right!

Finding the right person as your life partner requires care and patience. From this one decision will come ninety per cent of all your happiness or misery in life. It is said that love is blind. Many couples fall in love at the first sight. It is hard for them to be patient when they are looking for an intimate, romantic relationship. If you want to have a life-long relationship, don't be in haste. Don't ignore or deny the warning signs of trouble ahead - major differences in cultures, values, lifestyles, education, character and family backgrounds, etc. Physical attraction alone is not enough to make a happy marriage. "Any relationship primarily built on physical attraction is predestined to be short lived," said American writer and motivational speaker, Zig Ziglar.

Would you jump into water howsoever fresh and pristine, without knowing swimming or means of survival in water? I suppose, you won't. It is the same when you jump into a life long relationship without knowing your partner fully. Evaluate a potential partner with careful consideration to his or her character, personality, values, relationships with others, family history, and major cultural and lifestyle differences. Know your partner's beliefs about relationships. Different people have different and often conflicting beliefs about relationships. You don't want to fall in love with someone who expects lots of dishonesty and cheating in relationships. Don't confuse sex with love. Especially in the beginning of a relationship, attraction and pleasure in sex are often mistaken for love. Sometimes, influenced by physical attraction and lust for sex, you may ignore the major differences, and get into a marriage relationship hoping your partner will change or improve overtime. This is a recipe for disappointment, disaster. There is a Chinese saying which carries the meaning that "It is easier to reshape a mountain or a river than a person's character." Although, as an adult you are free to go the way you like, seeking opinion and advice from parents, close friends and well-wishers who may have wider experience and insight, can be helpful in taking the right decision about choosing your life partner.

There is a saying that a perfect match can only be found between a blind wife and a deaf husband, because the blind wife cannot see the faults of the husband and the deaf husband cannot hear the nagging of the wife. Yes, many would-be life partners are blind and deaf at the courting stage and dream of long-lasting perfect relationships. Unfortunately, when the excitement of romance wears off, they wake up and discover that marriage is not a bed of roses, as they imagined. And then the nightmare begins. A marriage is an agreement to spend a future together. So don't be impatient in choosing your life partner. Take a long-range view.

Mantras of a Successful Marriage

Success in marriage is more than finding the right partner. A successful marriage depends on the manner in which the relationship between the two individuals who have now become life partners is handled. A happy marriage is not a one-time affair, but requires continuous efforts to keep it that way. "A successful marriage," said Andre Maurois, the famous French author "is an edifice that must be rebuilt every day."

From the several unsuccessful love stories we came across during our search for building relationships, we found that lots of couples – new as well as seasoned, had no idea what a successful marriage even looks like.

Here are some of the most important mantras of a loving, stable and life-long marriage:

- Love your partner
- Respect and appreciate your partner
- Have trust in your partner
- Don't criticize or blame your partner
- Balance your family life
- Handle disagreements gracefully
- Honour your commitments
- Make mutual adjustments
- Share with your partner
- Grow with your partner

Love Your Partner

"Happy marriages begin, when we marry the ones we love and they blossom when we love the ones we marry," says Tom Mullen, the famous American singer and writer. Marriage is a sacred and satisfying relationship, which must be nurtured by love for each other. "A successful marriage requires falling in love many times, always with the same person," said journalist, author Mignon McLaughlin.

Love is the basis of a happy and long-lasting marriage. Without love, marriage will wither away soon. Marital love, which is called *prem* in Sanskrit, is a unique feeling, an emotional force that is much more profound and powerful than any other form of love. Besides love, compassion, respect, care and other feelings that are essential in all relationships, sex is a strong binding force in a marital relationship. Sex or lovemaking is not just a physical release but rather the sharing of love and pleasure, and the expression of a rich and full life. Lack of sex can ruin a marriage. Sexual incompletion leads to unhappiness and frustration among couples and is the principal cause of many broken marriages. So, make your love's romantic fire burning. How?

There are many practices in yoga that stimulate sex, make it stronger and fulfilling to both the partners. Many people have reported a general improvement in their health and sexual performance, and a happier life after being in yoga for a few months. A 40 years old hotel manager, who attended one of my yoga workshops in Mumbai, has this to say: "After practising yoga for about eight months, and following a strict diet, my weight reduced from 110 to 85 kg. Now, I feel very fit, and can do even the most difficult asana. I am six feet tall, and I am confident that continued practice of yoga will help me further reduce my weight to an ideal value for my height. Yoga has also improved my sexual potency, which has resulted in a very satisfying sex with my wife. This has improved our marital relations, and my wife adores me as an ideal husband."

I receive, perhaps you also, numerous e-mails in my junk mailbox on sex enhancement, Viagra, penis enlargement, erectile problems, etc. Don't get swayed away by these advertising gimmicks. They are not effective in increasing your sexual potency. Only good exercise, especially yoga practices and a healthy diet play an important role in one's sexual life.

A good, balanced diet increases one's sexual potency. The choice of diet is so wide that it is very difficult to say what to eat and what not. But certainly, fried, fatty foods are harmful for making effective sex. "Foods that keep the blood vessels in good condition help peg your body rich in testosterone hormone and estrogen (in females). These define your sexual potency," says Prakash Kothari, an expert sexologist.

Vegetarian food also rids you of lethargy and makes you sexually stronger. A US study found that one in four North American men was impotent by the age of 60, and blocked arteries were to be blamed for it. Eating meat clogs the arteries that travel to all organs of the body and affect our sexual potency. Research has also revealed that vegetarians need less sleep and have higher energy levels, which makes them appear more appealing in the bedroom.

More important than what you eat is, when you eat before the act of lovemaking? You can't enjoy sex with stomach full. When major chunk of your internal energy is being used in the process of digestion, where do you get the energy to fuel the sexual process that requires even more energy? You will get drained easily, and run short of energy to carry the sexual process to its successful completion. Yogic texts therefore, recommend allowing two to three hours for getting into the act of lovemaking after taking a hearty meal.

Drinking alcohol, smoking and taking drugs are bad habits anyway. Their use has a very bad effect on sex. Some people are under the wrong impression that a booze or smoke before sex will heighten their 'spirits' and give them a kick. Yes, you will surely be kicked-off much before you expected. Besides, their ill effects on the physiology of mind and body, the very smell of these intoxicants may repel the otherwise fully charged partners to be in intimate contact necessary for a good sex.

Further, as a married person, one is required to be loyal to one's spouse and refrain from illicit sex. Illicit sex outside of marriage is seen with disrespect as degeneration of human, moral and societal values. Leave aside morality and human values for a moment, even the modern medical science believes that AIDS and other sexually transmitted diseases are the byproducts of illicit-multi partner-rampant sex.

Respect and Appreciate Your Partner

"It is wrong to think that love comes from long companionship and persevering courtship. Love is the offspring of spiritual affinity and unless that affinity is created in a moment, it will not be created in years or even generations," said philosopher poet Kahlil Gibran in his book, *The Broken Wings*. How do we bring that affinity in our love?

Human beings crave intimacy. They look forward to being loved, cared, and respected. However, caught in the rut of daily routines, we take our partner for granted and forget to show our partner how much we truly appreciate him or her. Appreciation is the purest and strongest form of love that asks for nothing and gives everything.

Holding hands reflect deep feeling of love and care for the partner. Take notice of little things to say hello, good morning, how do you do, good-bye, I am sorry, please, excuse me, thank you, if you don't mind, I appreciate etc. These niceties and good manners are not only for third persons or strangers. Exchange these courtesies with your partner as often as possible. These are ways of demonstrating continued awareness and appreciation of another. You open the car door for a casual acquaintance (a lady!) as a matter of etiquettes, but when it comes to your own wife, you forget respect and courtesy. How strange!

Mutual respect is essential to a good relationship. It reflects the feeling and regard for each other. Give a loving kiss to your partner before leaving for work. Make efforts to greet the partner when he or she comes home from work. Don't insist on immediately talking about important matters, paying bills, pending repairs, a new purchase, kid's problems or something that needs attention. Ask your partner to share something good about his or her day.

Everyone loves to hear a compliment now and then. It makes us feel good about ourselves to have the approval or admiration of others. Praise and give compliments on his/

her twinkling eyes, gorgeous smile, generous heart, new dress, or some achievement. There are many ways you can express your appreciation and love for your partner: You look gorgeous, beautiful, I love you more than my life, I love you from all my heart and soul, I am so lucky to have you in my life, you mean everything to me, I miss you etc. Such expressions are music to your partner and he or she would love to hear them often. These words are not only to be found in etiquette books or to be spoken by lovers in a movie; they are for common use by every partner.

As human beings, we inevitably hurt each other, intentionally or unintentionally. If your partner hurts you, you have the choice of holding your resentment or forgiving. Forgiveness halts the cycle of blame and pain. If we forgive the others, others will ignore our mistakes too. By forgiving, you also loosen the feeling of guilt.

Many relationships fail because one partner tries to overpower the other, or demands too much from her or him. Instead of looking within ourselves to find who truly we are and what we desire, we often look to our partner to make us happy and whole. We try to change the behaviour of our partner instead of trying to change ourselves. Having high expectation on changing the partner's behaviour will cause disappointment and unpleasantness. It would be less painful to change ourselves and lower our expectations. So try to change yourself, not your partner. Mahatma Gandhi said, "We must be the change we wish to see in the world."

Trust Your Partner

Trust is the most important thing in all relationships, and more so in marriage. When trust is broken, it is the end of the relationship. Lack of trust leads to suspicion, suspicion generates anger, anger causes enmity and enmity may result in separation. "Trust is the glue of life. It is the most essential ingredient in effective communications. It's the foundational principle that holds all relationships," says Stephen R. Covey, the management guru.

A telephone operator received a phone call one day. She answered, 'Public Utilities Board.' There was silence. She repeated, 'PUB.' There was still no answer. When she was going to cut off the line, she heard a female voice, "Oh, so this is PUB. Sorry, I got the number from my husband's pocket but I do not know whose number it is."

Without mutual trust, just imagine what will happen to the couple if the telephone operator answered with just "hello" instead of "PUB".

And trust is built on honesty. If you are not true to your partner and tell lies, you are sowing the seeds of mistrust in the relationship. This reminds me of a young, newly married couple. The girl was not skilled in cooking except for a recipe of chicken biryani, which perhaps, she picked up from a cookery magazine. After a month or so of enjoying their honeymoon and invitations from near and dear ones, one day the girl cooked her recipe. At the dinner table, the girl asked the husband if he liked it. "Oh, yes darling! It is delicious." Actually he did not like the preparation at all, but knowing that she had taken a lot of interest and worked hard to make it, did not want to discourage her. The wife was happy and believing that he really liked it, cooked it very often.

Since she had no sense of proportioning the recipe for two of them, every time she cooked, lot was left over to be consumed the next day and perhaps, the next. The husband got fed up and one day in anger, threw the dish away and confessed that he hated her cooking. She was shocked and hurt. "I will never trust you. You are dishonest and told me lies," she said with tears in her eyes.

Don't Criticise or Blame Your Partner

A man asked his father-in-law, "Many people praised you for a successful marriage. Could you please share with me your secret?" The father-in-law answered with a smile, "Never criticize your wife for her shortcomings or when she does something wrong. Always bear in mind that because of her shortcomings and weaknesses, she could not find a better husband than you."

Very often, we have the habit of asking who is responsible or whom to blame, whether in a relationship, in a job or with the people we know. While responsibility and accountability are vital in a healthy relationship, unfair blame or criticism is toxic, especially when it comes to your life partner. We should always remember that when we point one finger at a person, the other four fingers point at ourselves. When a partner makes a mistake, he or she should not look around to find a scapegoat to point the finger at the other. This is the start of a war. Instead, take it easy, and don't blame or criticize your partner, instead appreciate him or her.

A boy was born to a couple after eleven years of marriage. They were a loving couple and the boy was the gem of their eyes. When the boy was around two years old, one morning the husband saw a medicine bottle open. He was late for office so he asked his wife to cap the bottle and keep it in the cupboard. His wife, preoccupied in the kitchen totally forgot the matter. The boy saw the bottle and playfully went to the bottle fascinated by its colour and drank it all. It happened to be a poisonous medicine meant for adults in small dosages. When the child collapsed the mother hurried him to the hospital, where he died. The mother was stunned. She was terrified how to face her husband. When the distraught father came to the hospital and saw the dead child, he looked at his wife and uttered just five words. The husband just said, "I am with you Darling".

The husband's totally unexpected reaction is a proactive behaviour. The child is dead. He can never be brought back to life. There is no point in finding fault with the mother. Besides, if only he felt more responsibility and had taken time to keep the bottle away, this would not have happened. No one is to be blamed. She had also lost her only child. What she needed at that moment was consolation and sympathy from the husband, and not blame. That is what he gave her.

Many relationships break off because of wrong speech. Therefore, mind your words. There is a Chinese saying, which carries the meaning that "A speech will either prosper or ruin a nation." When a couple is too close with each other, they often take each other for granted and say anything without considering if it would hurt the other person. Partners need to be polite. Relationship does not give you the license for rudeness.

A friend and her millionaire husband visited their construction site. A worker who wore a helmet saw her and shouted, "Hi, Emily! Remember me? We used to date in the secondary school." On the way home, her millionaire husband teased her, "Luckily you married me. Otherwise you will be the wife of a construction worker." She answered, "You should appreciate that you married me. Otherwise, he will be the millionaire and not you."

Another joke between a couple: "I would die for you, my love."

"Oh, Harry, you are always saying that, but you never do anything about it."

Many people have the habit of cutting cheap jokes or passing uncultured remarks about their partner in private or even in the presence of other people, may be to show they are smarter. This is insulting and hurts the feelings of the other partner. Exchanging such remarks frequently, especially, in public, sows the seed for a bad relationship. It's like a broken egg - cannot be reversed. Sir Winston Churchill, the noted British prime minister and his wife experienced one of the bitterest relationships in history. They always tried to pull each other down with sarcastic remarks.

Balance Your Family Life

A major cause of conflicts in marriage is the imbalance in work and family life. The highly competitive, overworked and stressful life of the present times is a big barrier to enjoy a great marriage. In the mad race to catch up with the changing times, we are losing track of what is important and in doing so we often sacrifice the values, which support our relationships. It is important we balance our careers and families for a successful marriage.

During the last few decades, because of various reasons, it has become quite common for both husband and wife to work and earn. This brings in the biggest imbalance in our work and family life. With dual career partners and the parenting demands, couples often complain of not getting enough time for each other. And if you and your spouse spend a great deal of time apart, due to different work shifts, schedules or frequent business tours, the time spent together may be even lesser. That can be a great challenge in your marital relationship.

If couples care for their marriage and want to enjoy it fully, it is essential they look seriously how they maintain a good balance in their family life and careers. They need to set their priorities right: happy family life or careers and lot of money. We are not saying that both the partners should not go to work, but they need to make certain basic changes in the way they are managing their lives. What options do they have?

First, let only one partner take up the mainstream career. The other stays home and manages the household. In addition, he or she can take up some secondary career operating from the home. In olden times, the husband, responsible for earning, went out to work while the wife looked after the home. This distribution of work between the couple may not be always feasible in the present social order where gender equality is the norm. Each couple has to see its convenience, skills and priorities to decide who goes out to work and who stays home.

Or, one of the partners takes a break from his or her career for a few years till the children become self-reliant. Here again, who should sacrifice career will depend on merit. If not mistaken for our gender-bias, we would suggest in most cases, it would be more fruitful for wife to make this sacrifice, because biologically mother is more suited to raise the offspring than the father. This is a God-made difference between a man and a woman and we should respect that in the fair distribution of work.

In our own case, though Indu was equally qualified and competent to continue in her career, and I am sure, if she had continued uninterrupted, she would have risen to a very high position. But she decided to work intermittently as the family responsibilities demanded. At the time of our marriage, she was working as a research scientist in All India Institute of Medical Sciences, New Delhi, but left the job after we had the first child and stayed home for about three years. She took up a teaching job for three-four years and again took a break when our second child arrived. After the second child was about four, she took up a research job in Lady Harding Medical College and Hospital. She left that job too after about ten years when I got a good job in the Caribbean. In this way, she gave more importance to my career, sacrificing hers without any grudge.

Another option for the couple would be to live in the combined family where their parents or other family members can look after the children as both the partners go for work. This arrangement can be possible only if the couple and their extended family are located at the same place, and the parents or other family members are willing and capable to look after the children.

Further, most couples are in hurry, in the fast lane, trying to fit more and more into the same fixed 24 hours to meet the grilling demands at work and home. At the end of the day, you are irritable, stressed out, and drained of energy. This can disrupt the relationship that may lead to a whole set of unrelated disputes over the most inconsequential stuff. If you look patiently, you wonder if it is all worth.

Therefore, learn to slowdown and relax. Spend as much time together as possible and have fun in life. Enjoy weekends with family eating out, meeting friends and families, going to movies, parks, exhibitions or other places of interest. A young couple was sleeping in the night when their smoke alarm went off. The husband jumped out of the bed, ran to the hall, and then back to the bedroom. "Get up honey, evacuate, there is a fire in the house." Quickly he led her out of the house to safety. As they looked at the cloud of smoke coming from the house, he noticed a smile on her face. "The house is burning, what is there to smile about," he said taking a big sigh. "I can't help it, she replied. It is the first night we've gone out together in five years!"

Don't be like the above couple. Avail your vacations and go to places – mountains, beaches, whatever interests you and your family. Remember that except for rare life-and-death matters, nothing is as important as it first seems. You may ask yourself if the sky will fall down, if someone will die, or if the world will stop spinning if you take vacation from work to rest, recreate, spend time with family and go out on holidays to feel peaceful.

Handle Disagreements Gracefully

Small disputes and disagreements are quite normal in relationships. A relationship with no differences or challenges could be dull. Disagreements or disputes can happen on many issues, and the partners should learn to resolve them with love and mutual understanding. Disagreements don't sink relationships. Calling names or abusing each other does!

Usually, the matters are not serious – there is more salt in the food, tea is too strong, something is misplaced, child did some wrong – sort of things which can be handled with mutual trust and understanding. However, if not handled properly, these simple issues may turn volatile with anger or tension reaching a boiling point from where the situation can go totally out of control.

> In disagreement with your spouse, deal only with the current situation. Don't bring up the past.

But remember not to try to resolve a dispute even if it is serious when tempers are high and partners are mad. You may make the situation even worse. In such a situation, instead of dragging the arguments indefinitely, the best approach is to take a break, and walk away, mutually agreeing to discuss the matter later. Take time to cool down and let the storm of rage blow off. Go out, breathe deeply, do some *pranayama*, watch nature, and relax. This will soothe your soul and your mind will be more open and clear. And most of the times the things would get resolved by themselves.

Did you know that emperor Akbar had instructed his ministers not to carry out his orders immediately? They were asked to wait till the emperor repeated his order. This was to give a cooling time in case he said something in anger the first time.

Anger is madness in which one can do anything. We have a young couple in our neighbourhood. We knew that the husband, an MBA and general manager in a retail store was very short tempered, but did not know how far he could go mad with his wife. One day, I saw the wife with a swollen eye and asked her if there was anything wrong. Initially she was secretive, but later confided in me that her husband often beat her mercilessly on small disputes, even in presence of their teenage daughter, and pleaded that I talk to him. I tried to exhort the youngman, but he would not listen. Finally, I said to him, "Rakesh, if not for your wife, at least think of Anita, your teenage daughter. You are going to give her in marriage, say after ten years, and how would you feel if her husband beat her like you do to your wife." "How anybody dare beat my loving daughter?" he replied.

"You said it right. Is not your wife the loving daughter of her father?" I questioned. He was quiet and seemingly moved by my words, promised to behave.

Silence is the best antidote to anger. A couple used to quarrel over small issues, as both of them were very short tempered. One day, the wife went to a saint and asked for some remedy for her anger. The saint gave her a bottle of some medicine and advised her to put a few drops in her mouth without swallowing, whenever she was angry. That evening, the couple had an angry bout over some issue, and the wife took the medicine as prescribed by the saint. Fearing she may swallow or spill the medicine, she kept her mouth shut. Things calmed down. Next day, she again went to the saint and told him that the medicine worked wonders and requested for some more. The saint said, "that was no medicine, it was just plain water, which kept you quiet when you held it in your mouth."

Whenever your partner is angry, try to keep your serenity. Listening is a great antidote for anger. Listen to your partner's concerns and complaints without judgement. Much of the time, just having someone listen is all we need for solving problems. Also it opens the door to confiding. During these times, empathy is very crucial. Look at things from your partner's perspective as well as your own. Contemplate on "what is so wrong with me that made my partner so angry. What can I do to change myself? How can I get him or her to love me?" Holding on to anger, hurt or pain only wastes your energy and keeps you away from love.

Anyone can make mistakes. No one wants to be told they are wrong. No one wants to hear that their behaviour is putting themselves and others they love to danger. Whenever you or your spouse makes a mistake, regardless of who is wrong, apologize. Say, "I am sorry, I upset you." These are healing, magical words that will bury the hatch and prevent the matter to escalate.

If you have children, it is not uncommon to have differences over parenting styles and bringing up children.

For instance, you may want to spoon feed the child, whereas your husband wants the child to be independent and feed for itself. You may want the child to go to a public school but your husband prefers private schooling for the child. Again one of the parents may prefer a hard-line, strict disciplinary style, while the other may have a subtler, friendly approach. Both have their pros and cons. Try to understand each other's views and let these small differences not affect your relationship.

Make Mutual Adjustments

Marriage always puts many demands on both partners for mutual adjustments and understanding, especially if they are from different cultures or family background. It is quite likely they may have lot of differences in habits, tastes, likes and dislikes, and lifestyle, etc. In married life, you need to compromise on certain issues which you may not really like or enjoy. Marriage is an orchestra; enjoy it being in harmony. Appreciate your partner's differences and make small adjustments. One should learn to accommodate the other's likes and dislikes with love and concern. Intimacy is bound to develop with such readiness to accommodate.

I recall the initial years of our own marriage. I had a poor sense of personal hygiene with respect to dental care and clothing. I appreciate how Indu, with her loving and caring concern made me brush twice a day, once in the morning and the other before going to bed, and convinced me to change my dress, especially undergarments every day. Again, she inculcated in me the habit of using deodorant regularly to get rid of the foul small of perspiration.

Over the time my concern for dental care grew so strong that I did everything possible to keep the teeth healthy and fresh. I started using *neem* twig for cleaning my teeth in the morning and brushing with toothpaste in the night. Though *neem* is excellent for protecting teeth from bacterial infections and foul small, and it showed its good effect on me, Indu was not convinced about its efficacy. Many years later when she had some tooth problem, she took my advice to try *neem* with good result. Ever since, both of us use *neem* twigs in the morning and brush in the evening for keeping our teeth clean. Our teeth all in tact, are sparkling white, and beautiful till this age also (69 years for me and 65 for Indu).

Again, both of us had wide differences in tastes. She was fond of spicy food whereas I could not tolerate chillies. I was fond of vegetarian food and she liked non-vegetarian. It took both of us a little time to change our tastes, but there was no ill feeling or arrogance.

Honour Your Commitments

Marriage ceremonies in many cultures include rituals where the wedding couples make commitments and take vows to keep their promises in their wedlock, in presence of priests, relatives and friends as witnesses. But alas! Partners forget those promises very soon. How nice it would be if you honour your vows daily, rather than just on that special ceremonial occasion. Do you remember what oaths you took, what commitments and promises you made at your marriage ceremonies? Keep those promises and commitments always alive.

On the occasion of his golden anniversary, a newspaper correspondent asked Albert Einstein: "Sir, what is the secret of your successful marriage?" Professor Einstein answered, "When we first got married, we made a pact that I would make all the big decisions and my wife would make all the little decisions. For fifty years, we have held true to that agreement. I believe that is the reason of success in our marriage. However, the strange thing is that in fifty years, there hasn't been one big decision!"

Remember your partner's birthdays, wedding anniversary and other important occasions of your married life and celebrate them with love and enthusiasm. How Mukesh Ambani celebrated his wife Nita's 44th birthday with a custom-built $500 million jet plane with a promise of gifting her a Rs. 5000 crore, 27 storeyed house in Mumbai on her next birthday, may not be your way. And you may not also present Imperial Majesty No.1, the world's most expensive perfume that costs $215,000 for a 500ml bottle to your wife on her birthday, but don't forget to wish her a happy birthday with a gorgeous kiss and of course, a lovely, affordable gift.

For her birthday, Victoria Beckham reportedly received a necklace studded with diamonds, rubies and sapphires worth $8 million from footballer husband David Beckham. He also flew out a team of top chefs from London to cook food for her in Spain. After three kids, some couples may find it hard to keep such spark in their romance, but not the Beckhams!

Share with Your Partner

An old couple walked slowly into a McDonald's one cold winter evening. They looked out of place amid the young families and young couples eating there that night. Some of the customers looked admiringly at them. You could tell what the admirers were thinking: "Look, there is a couple who has been through a lot together, probably for 60 years or more!"

The old man walked up to the cash register, placed his order with no hesitation and then paid for their meal. The couple took a table near the back wall and started taking food off the tray. There was one hamburger, one order of French fries and one drink.

The old man unwrapped the hamburger and carefully cut it in half. He placed one half in front of his wife. Then he carefully counted out the French fries, divided them in two piles and neatly placed one pile in front of his wife. He took a sip of the drink, and then his wife took a sip as the man began to eat his few bites. Again, you could tell what people around the old couple were saying. "They were used to sharing everything."

Then the crowd noticed that the little old lady still hadn't eaten a thing. She just sat there watching her husband eat and occasionally sipped some of the drink. A young man came over and begged them to let him buy them another meal. The lady explained that no, they were used to sharing.

As the old man finished eating and was wiping his face neatly with a napkin, the young man could stand it no longer and asked again. After being politely refused again, he finally asked the old lady, "Ma'am, why aren't you eating. You said that you share everything. What is it that you are waiting for?" "The Teeth," she answered

Well, you may not share dentures or spectacles with your partner, but there are lots of other things in relationship that you need to share. In fact, relationships work only when they are two-way streets, with much give and take. Share all your secrets, your moments of happiness and sorrow with your partner. Confide in your partner, as no one else understands your needs and limitations better as he or she. Your partner is a great source of strength in your difficult times.

And wait! How about sharing household responsibilities! If you are not involved in the household chores, you may not even know how difficult it is to manage home-affairs. Sharing household activities, especially when both the partners are working and there are kids at home, is very essential to maintain cordial relations in the family. Indifference or selfishness of partners in sharing the household responsibilities is often the cause of many marital conflicts.

In places where household help is available, the situation may not be that tough, but in most places, especially in developed societies such help is not affordably available, and unless both the partners share the household responsibilities, it may be very hard and frustrating for one partner to manage the home. It may be a good idea for the partners to make a list of various household activities, even the most mundane ones, and share these among themselves as per their skills, capabilities, limitations, and convenience. A typical list of household activities, certainly not the complete one, may look like this: Buying groceries from the store, washing vegetables and fruits, cooking food, buying cooked food from outside, washing dishes, doing laundry, Ironing clothes, making beds, cleaning and sweeping the house, cleaning toilets, putting garbage for disposal, cleaning children, bathing and dressing children, dropping kids at school, bringing kids from school, taking kids to activities, writing checks and paying bills, and so on and so forth.

The list is unending. One of our friends, a former managing director of a large oil refinery often remarked, "It is easier to manage the list of inventories in a refinery than to comprehend what you may require at home."

There are numerous other ways partners can share their interests, hobbies and other special talents that bring them closer to each other. For instance, writing this book together gave us immense feeling of sharing and cooperation. It involved a lot of valuable dialogue and discussion that deepened our connection and brought us closer. May be this effort inspires other couples to cultivate the richness of sharing in their own relationship.

Grow With Your Partner

"Love at first sight is easy to understand; it's when two people have been looking at each other for a lifetime that it becomes a miracle," said Sam Levenson, the famous American TV host. But, our promise is that if couples sincerely apply the forgoing mantras of happy marriage, a lifelong relationship may not be a miracle, but a reality.

Our relations with others in the family may change with time, but the sacred relationship between a husband and wife is eternal. Partners always need each other, but much so as they grow older. Your sweet heart is the best companion you can ever have. Indian born, writer and activist, Arthur F. Lenehan gave this advice to all brides, "If any of you happen to marry an archeologist, you're in luck. The older you get, the more he'll be interested in you." Poor brides! Don't lose heart. Try to find that archeologist in your groom.

Love your partner even more than you loved him or her when you were younger. It is never being too old to hold hands. "You don't stop loving because you grow old. You grow old because you stop loving," said someone. Don't take your partner for granted. Keep yourself well dressed, attractive and adorable to your partner, no matter what your age. And remember love is not always for lust, sex, and sensual pleasures. It is much more profound and sacred. It reflects the feeling and regard for each other. Be with your partner as much as possible, and try to do things together. Sharing common interests and participating in each other's activities brings closeness.

Fortunate are the couples that live together till a ripe old age. Pray that you live with your partner together forever, for *saat janam*. You are helpless if death takes away your partner, but why you strain and sever the relationship deliberately by your wrong and selfish attitudes.

We lived in South America for many years. A Latin American friend of ours invited us for a get-together in his home on a Sunday. I expressed difficulty in accepting his invitation due to a prior engagement. When he insisted that we should come to his home, I pleaded that we had to go to one of our Indian friends who was hosting a party on the sixtieth wedding anniversary of his parents. "What did you say? Sixtieth wedding anniversary! Are you kidding? How come a man live with the same woman for sixty long years?" he asked curiously. I had a hard time convincing my Latin friend about the integrity of Indian marriages. It was strange for him to believe that marriage in India was a sacred institution, and not a short-term legal contract.

One of our doctor friends narrated this incident that made him know what is true love or *pyar ho to aisa:* It was a busy morning, about 8:30, when an elderly gentleman in his 80's arrived in the hospital to have stitches removed from his thumb. He said he was in a hurry as he had an appointment at 9:00 am. I took his vital signs and had him take a seat, knowing it would be over an hour before someone would be able to see him. I saw him looking at his watch and decided, since I was not busy with another patient, I would evaluate his wound. On examination, it was well healed, so I talked to one of the doctors, got the needed supplies to remove his sutures and redress his wound.

While taking care of his wound, I asked him if he had another doctor's appointment this morning, as he was in such a hurry. The gentleman told me no, that he needed to go to the nursing home to eat breakfast with his wife. I inquired as to her health. He told me that she had been there for a while and that she was a victim of Alzheimer's disease. As we talked, I asked if she would be upset if he was a bit late. He replied that she no longer knew who he was, that she had not recognised him in five years now. I was surprised, and asked him, "And you still go every morning, even though she doesn't know who you are?"

He smiled as he patted my hand and said, "She doesn't know me, but I still know who she is." I had to hold back tears as he left, I had goose bumps on my arm, and thought, "That is the kind of love I want in my life." True love is neither physical, nor romantic. True love is an acceptance of all that is, has been, will be, and will not be.

Think Before Breaking Up

Remember the quote in the beginning of this chapter. Yes, partners are the pair of shears that have to be held together. Love, acceptance, understanding and sensitivity to the other person's needs form the rivet that holds the shears together and allows them to work interdependently. But what happens when the rivet fails, shears are not aligned or rusted; the marriage fails.

American television journalist, Bob Phillips describes love as a three-ring circus. First comes the engagement ring, then the wedding ring, and after that the suffering. Are you in the last ring of the circus that you want to get away? Fighting, separating or divorce has never solved anybody's problems; they have only helped lawyers and consultants. Don't get lured by the hefty awards given by courts to divorcees like Britain's pop star Paul McCartney and actress wife Heather Mills (pounds 50 million), US basketball great Michael Jordan and wife Juanita ($168 million) or others. Litigations might have given celebrity divorcees a lot of money plus fame and popularity they needed more, however, they will give only pain and miseries to most divorcing couples.

"It takes two to make a marriage a success and only one to make it a failure," said British diplomat, Herbert Samuel. Are you the main actor behind the failed marriage? Reflect on your bad relationship and use it as a mirror to look at yourself, to understand what in you is creating this relationship.

If we carefully examine it's not the big problems that cause a marriage to fail. It is rather a series of small things smoldering over a long time that blow off a relationship. Think over these small things in day-to-day life: Am I always complaining, demanding, arrogant, fault-finding, blaming, ridiculing, ordering, manipulating, unkind, disrespectful, and so on, but still consider myself as a loving partner. Too often, we believe that marriage gives us the license to indulge in inconsiderate behaviour, thoughtlessness or even rudeness, which ultimately ruins a relationship.

An accident happens not because of one reason, but many things go wrong that cause the accident. The same is true of a failed marriage. Carefully examine all the underlying causes of your bad relationship. A good marriage creates so many points of contact between two souls that severance of all connections would mean the derangement of practically the whole purpose of life. Contemplate on your behaviour. Learn to bend; it is better than breaking.

And don't be in haste in severing your relationship. Don't just run away from a bad marriage; you may only repeat it with the next partner, or perhaps even worse. So think, not once or twice, but several times before breaking up. Seek advice of wise people who understand life better, and try to change yourself before you change your relationship.

In a lighter vein: Have you ever noticed how all of women's problems start with MEN? Carefully examine the composition of the following words:

> MEN tal illness
> MEN strual cramps
> MEN tal breakdown
> MEN opause
> GUY necologist

But also see below how man and woman are joined with each other that you can't separate them:

> Woman has Man in it;
> Mrs. has Mr. in it;
> Female has Male in it;
> She has He in it;
> Madam has Adam in it;

5

Art of Parenting

> The joys of parents are secret, and so are their griefs and fears.
>
> *Francis Bacon*

From the institution of marriage you have graduated to enter the world of parenthood. Welcome to this new relationship. Being a mother or father is a great feeling, which you experience only when you become one. Parenthood is an inner change, so profound and intense we ourselves grow in it. It is not only children who grow, but parents also.

Parents are like weavers who join the threads of the past with the threads of the future leaving the legacy of their own beautiful loving patterns as they go. It is said that you are the reflection of the lives of your parents, and their parents, and theirs. Now, being parents yourselves, remember the sacrifices and blessings bestowed by your parents to you, and with a feeling of gratitude, give the same to your children.

Parenting is one of the most challenging, demanding and stressful jobs, yet most parents love to undertake it. Samuel G. Goodrich, the nineteenth century American author put this paradox of parenting, this way: "How many hopes and fears, how many ardent wishes and anxious apprehensions are twisted in the threads that connect the parent with the child."

Volumes have been written on parenting which give useful information and guidelines on how to raise or bring up children, but what can't be found in these books is the inner experience of parenting - love, compassion and care. "According to me parenting requires us to consciously engage ourselves in an inner search as well as in the outer experience of caring for our children. The 'how-to' advice that we can draw from books has to be complemented by an inward authority that we should cultivate within ourselves through our experiences", says Padma Bhushan, Dr. Shyama Chona, former principal of Delhi Public School, in an interview in *The Times of India*.

Parents shape, or misshape, their children depending on how they bring them up. Remember: Tomorrow's world will be shaped by what we teach our children today. Parents can learn a lot from nature, which teaches us the virtue of nurture, not command and control. Here are some parenting guidelines reflecting this principle of nurture.

Love Your Children

Nurture your children with love, care and compassion. Nurturing children we wonder, who is nurturing whom? Children are great teachers. They stop you up short, shake you up, and wake you up. They keep you on your toes and help you regain your sense of humor and playfulness. Some parents may be blessed with wisdom or lot of riches. Others know the meaning of patience and hard work. Still others may have lot of comforts and conveniences. But what matters most in parenting is to know how much love, how many hugs and kisses you can shower on your children.

Parent's love for their children is called *vatsalya* in Sanskrit, which is a great feeling that can't be explained in words. Only the heart of a parent, especially the mother can feel *vatsalya*. Babies who are well cared for may find in feeding time the roots of comfort and pleasure, hope and optimism, trust and whatever other ingredients go into the feeling we call *vatsalya*. Show your love by touching, caressing, kissing, hugging and massaging. "Always kiss your children good night – even if they're asleep," said H. Jackson Brown, Jr., a best selling American author.

In villages, the cows go out in the fields for grazing leaving their small calves at home. In the evening when they return home, they are so overwhelmed with love for their offsprings that milk oozes out from their breasts. As a mother, do you have the same feeling for your little ones?

Know Your Children's Needs

As a parent, we must be attentive to the needs of our children. It is important to understand what young children expect from us as parents. Don't worry that you can't give your kids the best of everything. Give them your very best. I received a beautiful 'e-mail forward' from a friend in which a child is expressing its needs as Ten Commandments to its parents. These commandments, in fact, summarize all what children generally expect from their parents.

- My hands are small, please don't expect perfection whenever I make a bed, draw a picture or throw a ball. My legs are short; please slow down so that I can keep up with you.
- My eyes have not seen the world as yours have, please don't expect me to see things the way you do.
- I am only little for a short time, please take time to explain things to me about this wonderful world.

- Don't scold me for my inquisitiveness. Treat me, as you would like to be treated.
- I am a special gift from God; please treasure me as God intended you to do, disciplining me in a loving manner.
- I need your encouragement to grow. You can criticize the things I do without criticizing me.
- Permit me to fail, so that I can learn from my mistakes.
- Please don't do things over for me. And please don't compare me to my brother or sister.
- Please don't be afraid to leave for a weekend together. Kids need vacations from parents, just as parents need vacations from kids.
- Please set a good example for me to follow. I enjoy learning.

Young children are curious to know many things of life, mundane or otherwise. They ask questions, sometimes little awkward for parents to answer. For example, when a child first asks where babies come from, the chances are that all he or she needs is very simple answer. A father, for instance, might reply, "Babies grow inside their mothers." It can also be a good idea to find out what answers our children have already imagined for themselves by asking, "Where do you think you came from?" Gently bringing their fantasies more in line with their reality may be all we need to do for a while. As they become comfortable with whatever new information we've given them, they'll let us know they're ready for more by asking again.

Be Patient with Children

Children make mistakes, and they will. But they need to be handled patiently. Overreacting and taking actions while in rage will haunt you forever. Read this story of a father who got mad on his little boy for nothing so significant:

A man came out of his home to admire his new car. To his utter surprise, he saw his four-year-old son happily hammering dents into the shiny paint of the truck. Furious, the man ran to his son, knocked him away, and hammered the little boy's hands as punishment.

When the father calmed down, he rushed his son to the hospital. Although the doctor tried desperately to save the crushed bones, he finally had to amputate the fingers from boy's both hands. When the boy woke up from the surgery and saw his bandaged stubs, he innocently said," Daddy, I'm sorry about your car." Then he asked, "But when are my fingers going to grow back?"

The father went home and committed suicide. Think about this story the next time your child does some wrong, or something you don't approve of. Think first before you lose your patience with someone you love. Cars can be repaired. Broken bones and hurt feelings often can't. We should be patient with children and forgive them when they make mistakes, or do something we don't like.

Rarely, there may be a parent who has not lost his or her temper. But getting mad like the father in the above story is an extreme behaviour and not called for. Be kind to your children even at times if you are angry with them. In anger, you might say some harsh words or resort to mild physical hurt. But after the heat of the moment has passed, it is good to apologize for something you did that was inappropriate. It's a good discipline (for us, as well as for our children) to be able to say, "I am sorry I got angry, and I shouldn't have hit you. The famous journalist and author, Mignon McLaughlin, wrote in her book, 'The Second Neurotic Notebook': "A parent who has never apologised to his children is a monster. If he's always apologising, his children are monsters."

Disciplining Children

Of course, children need to be disciplined if they are 'monsters', misbehave or do something that is disagreeable. "If a child annoys you, quieten him by brushing his hair. If this does not work, use the other side of the brush on the other end of the child," said someone. At such times you should be strict and firm with the child and show that you don't like his or her behaviour, but there is no need to be impatient and yell. You can still be nice in dealing with the child. By shouting unnecessarily you rather make the child more defiant, besides  losing your own grace and poise. Allow me to share an old incidence of a mother's yelling over her small boy, which is still fresh in my mind.

While I was working in the Caribbean in 1990s, I used to fly to Caracas quite often for official work. On one of my return trips from Caracas to Curacao, a young mother with a child (may be 3-4 years old) boarded the plane. She sat on the row in front of me. The young lady was extremely beautiful, well dressed, groomed and apparently looked educated and cultured. As kids do, little Peter was meddling with the things around. Suddenly, the mother shouted so loudly, "No, Peter, don't do this" that all the passengers in the 24-seater plane were wondering what happened. When little Peter did not stop, she gave a big slap on his face. During the entire half-an hour flight, the mother kept yelling, scolding and abusing the child. Her crude, uncivilized behaviour overshadowed her otherwise beautiful appearance. I overheard many passengers saying "What a beast?"

I have narrated this story to many young parents to remind them how they blemish their dignity, beauty and grace by their uncultured behavior with their kids, especially in the presence of others. So, if you care for your good looks, don't yell over your kids while disciplining them. And if you do yell, take the advice of the famous comedian and TV actor, Bill Cosby, who said: "Always end the name of your child with a vowel, so that when you yell, the name will carry."

Disciplining a child is not commanding, yelling or abusing. It involves love, care, and nurture, passing on traditions and values, and praise for achievement. Children learn from examples including your own. The examples of animals are very fascinating to young children. Make use of these while teaching them good behaviour.

Setting limits or boundaries for their children are one of the most important ways parents can regulate their children's behaviour, and help them become self-regulating adults. Set their boundaries – when and how much to play, what and how much TV to watch, how far from home to go out alone, what toys to play with and what not, and so on – and give them the freedom to work within these limits without meddling into their affairs. Some supervision is ok, but over-supervision or interference can cause you headache, besides making the child less reliant as he or she grows up. That is why the famous author, Susan Savannah advises: If your kids are giving you a headache, follow the directions on the aspirin bottle, especially the part that says, "Keep away from children."

During the last summers we visited our son and daughter-in-law who live in Chicago. Our four years old grand daughter, Mia often rode her bicycle on the sidewalk in front of her house. Initially, we were afraid she might go on the road, but we were surprised to see how she biked within the bounds laid by her father. Her limit was about 150 feet long stretch of that 4-feet wide sidewalk that she followed faithfully. We realised how laying limits and then giving them the freedom to act could discipline children. Try this with your children; it works.

A family is like an orchestra; we must play in harmony especially when disciplining the children. When one parent is dealing with the child to discipline him or her, the other parent should not interfere in the deal. Parents may have difference of opinion in their styles of bringing up or disciplining their children, but they should refrain from expressing these differences in front of the children when they are being tutored or reprimanded for doing something disagreeable.

Let us share with you the example of our young friend, John, to illustrate what happens when the parents show their differences openly in disciplining their children. Their five-year old daughter, Julie is very naughty. Whenever she does something wrong, our friend John, takes her aside in a corner of the house and tutors her softly but firmly to discipline her. Julie understands the tutoring and promises to behave. But Rina, his wife often, intervenes and tells John not to be hard with the child. This offsets any good effect John's talk has had on Julie. The result: Julie is not improving in her behaviour. Sometimes, even they receive complaints from her kindergarten school about her misbehaviour. John and Rina were worried about Julie's development. After the couple asked for our advice, we told them to follow the principle of harmony in disciplining the child. Of late Julie is showing marked improvement in her behaviour, and the couple seems to be happier.

Inculcate Values

Children are the heart and soul of the next generation and our hopes of a better tomorrow. As parents, it should be our responsibility to help our children develop holistically, so that they grow as responsible and caring adults to meet the challenges of the rapidly changing world of today. For this we need to implant core values - honesty, integrity, compassion, empathy, tolerance, humility and hard work, in our children right from a very young age. It is these fundamental values, which will last a lifetime.

Encourage children to follow the golden rule that says, "Cleanliness is next to godliness". Children should be taught to exercise personal hygiene, cleanliness of surroundings, and care for environment. Have children clean up from one activity before starting the next. Encourage them not to waste water and other materials, and save electricity. Encourage the concept of green environment and help them to grow as responsible environmental stewards.

Nurture their spiritual life. Encourage children to pray, meditate or practice yoga. Encourage them to spend time in nature and learn art forms like dance, music, painting, etc.

Many children struggle with self-esteem and doubt as they grow. Work hard to create in your children a good self-image. It's the most important thing you can do to ensure their success. Help them develop as confident, self-respecting persons by offering them genuine praise and encouragement whenever required. Let your children overhear you saying nice things about them to other adults.

Encourage the virtue of non-violence. Discourage fighting and violent activities among children. Don't let them watch violent TV shows, and buy the products that sponsor them. Don't let them intentionally hurt other people's feelings.

Teach your children the value of money and the importance of saving and thrift. Let the children not take for granted all the comforts and luxuries provided by parents. Teach children the importance of hard work. You handicap your children by making their lives easy.

Teach children to be self-reliant. Let children learn to do their tasks independently. Don't spoon-feed them. Don't do their homework or other assignments and projects of the school; guide them if necessary. "If you want children to keep their feet on the ground, put some responsibility on their shoulders," said Abigail Van Buren, contemporary American writer.

Encourage an attitude of respect, devotion and obedience. Reinforce these qualities through your own example. Children are very sensitive; they watch you how you behave with their grand parents and other elders in the family or society. If you are respectful and obedient they will follow you.

Encourage children to serve others at home and school. Encourage children to bring happy, loving energy to others. Do not tolerate complaining, arguing, interrupting, or disrespectful speech.

Teach children the value of family traditions, customs and rituals right from a young age. Erik Erikson, the great authority on child development, once said, "Traditions is to human beings what instinct is to animals. Imagine what would happen if animals lost their instinct! So you can imagine how our traditions need to be considered with respect."

Walk the Talk

There are no universities or colleges that offer degrees in parenting. We learn it by experience.

As a parent, you like to inculcate ideal principles into your children. All these lessons - the chores have to be done before play; cleanliness and good eating habits are aspects of self-esteem; speak truth; anger can be expressed through words and nondestructive activities; keep promises, don't break them; be compassionate, and so on - children can learn far more easily through the living example of their parents than they ever can through formal instructions. Children are like monkeys who act like their parents despite every effort to teach them good manners.

Sam, our nephew, with wife Rita and four-year-old daughter Rosy, lives close to our home. We visit them quite often. One Sunday, they had invited us for dinner. When it came to drinks, Sam and Rita poured wine in their glasses while Indu and I settled for lemonade. As we were gossiping and enjoying the drinks, Rita and Sam had to discipline little Rosy time and again not to meddle with the drinks. After a few sips, as Rita praised the wine, "Oh, really, it is very tasty, can I have some more," the little Rosy said curiously, "Mama, how does it taste like? Can I have some?" "No, sweetie, kids are not allowed to drink," said Rita authoritatively.

I could not resist making a comment that you should not talk so much about the wine, or better not take it when small children are around. "But uncle, we told her that kids don't drink alcohol. She is supposed to learn and behave. You want us not to have any fun because children are around." Rita reacted sharply.

You must walk the talk. There is no better way to demonstrate and set an example than by just exhorting your kids to do this or not do that. But if you think setting a good example for your children takes all the fun out of life, then you are selfish, and have not learnt the art of parenting. Setting examples for children requires some sacrifice. As parents, you should live so that when your children think of fairness, caring, trust, integrity, and other values, they think of you. "There comes a time when a woman needs to stop thinking about her looks and focus her energies on raising her children. This time comes at the moment of conception. A child needs a role model, not a supermodel," said Astrid Alauda.

Handling Teenagers

Handling teenagers has always been a difficult phase of parenthood. Adolescence brings with it a host of physiological and psychological changes in children when they need special care, counsel and comfort of the parents. They have problems and queries that need to be addressed by parents patiently and intelligently. Parents need to be very careful in dealing with children during this phase of life. Children need parents' love and understanding for facing the odds of adolescence.

It is also the time when children (of 12-21 years, though 13-19 is literally the teenage) need us not only for love and trust; they also need us for honest differing. This differing may not be only over limits and rules, or do's and don'ts that parents prescribe for their teenagers; it may also be differing about some of  what we have in the way of culture, tradition, and values. Parents can only give good advice or put them on the right paths, but the final forming of the youngsters' character lies in their own hands.

Unfortunately, this differing in culture, traditions, values and beliefs has taken youngsters on a totally different path during the last couple of decades. In the turmoil of the present times, influenced by materialism, consumer technology, individualism and hurried lifestyle, handling teenagers has become a nightmare for most parents. It gives parents headache and sleepless nights, as they do not know how to cope with it. The normal parenting skills are unable to deal with the youths, who are influenced more by peer pressures, media, glamour, reckless fashion, reality shows, and consumer electronics. Many parents are worried and weary of their teenagers getting increasingly involved in drinking, drugs, rave parties, Internet-porn, sex and other juvenile crimes. "A child today faces more sexual signals and temptations on the way to school than his grandfather did on Saturday night when he was looking for them", said Josh McDowell, contemporary US writer and evangelist.

The acts and echoes of crime, aggression, violence, war, terrorism and sex define the times we live in. They bombard our media, fill our newspapers and magazines, and overwhelm our 24x7 television sets. Our movies show rampant sex, violence, and other immoral acts. All this has very bad effect on the minds of people, especially the teenagers, who get mislead and lured to follow unethical lifestyles.

Teenagers are increasingly involved in juvenile crimes. One often comes across cases of teenagers shooting in schools and colleges, killing people by reckless driving, indulging in pornography, drugs and drinking, rave parties, road rages, immoral sex and other juvenile crimes. Till recently, I had only heard, read in the newspapers or watched on TV stories of teenage crimes, but I was taken aback when I was attacked by a group of teenagers during our visit to Chicago last year.

One day, I was taking my usual evening walk on the park trail close to our son's home in suburban Chicago. I noticed some 7 or 8 young Afro-American boys coming from the opposite direction. When they came across me, one boy asked me what the time was. I looked at my wristwatch and told it was half past six. Another boy asked the time again, pointing to his ears as if he did not hear me. I told again it was half past six and moved on. I would have walked hardly a few steps when one boy came hurriedly to me and started hitting on my face. In shock, I fell down and broke my glasses. I got up painfully and asked him the reason, but he kept punching me all over my body while the other boys were enjoying the fun. In terror, I ran for my life to the park where my wife, granddaughter and a few other parents were playing with their children. Not afraid of anybody, the boys followed me to the park. Everybody was surprised to see me bleeding and crying in pain. When my wife and some other people asked the boys why did they hit me, they point blank refused having done anything. Afraid of any untoward rivalry in the community, no body informed the police, and we being strangers did not know what to do.

However, on reaching home when my son and daughter-in-law heard my story, they informed the police. A police officer came immediately but showed his helplessness to take any firm steps. He said that such incidents involving teenagers from certain communities happen there quite often and the authorities are afraid to take any extreme step as it may incite youngsters to retaliate.

Reckless sex education is another irritant that is derailing the youngsters and embarrassing the parents. No doubt, sex education to youngsters is important, but the way our government, media and other interest groups are trying to educate the masses is ill conceived and badly implemented. Every day we notice a number of messages that are put up on huge billboards at prominent locations, and advertised through TV, newspapers, magazines and other media to educate people on family planning and safe sex.

Many of these messages are obscene and unethical in nature, which give wrong signals to the small children who also see them, rather more minutely. Once, I was driving my seven-year old granddaughter to school, when she saw a message on a big roadside billboard that reads, 'Go with condom'. She asked me innocently, "Nana, what is condom and are we carrying it." What should have I told her? It was so embarrassing. Somehow, I diverted her attention to some other topic, and saved the situation.

But how many times you can do that. Today, watching TV with family that can be otherwise so entertaining and educative, has become a curse. Most TV programmes, especially the commercial breaks are full of obscenity, violence, crime, and destruction, which are distracting and misleading to the youngsters and embarrassing for the parents to watch together. So are our newspapers, magazines and other media products full of stuff that lure the youngsters to follow immoral path. Sylvia Boorstein, the founding teacher at Spirit Rock Meditation Center, California wrote in an article on non-violence that appeared in the 'Yoga Journal'. "I limit my daily news intake to one newspaper; I don't watch TV, and I rarely listen to radio."

TV, newspapers, magazines, internet, movies, cell phones and others are far too many external forces distracting and tempting youngsters to follow immoral ways. Sometimes, I wonder whether the people who, because of their vested commercial interests, are damaging innocent lives of our youngsters, don't have their own children. Should not they exercise caution, discretion and better taste?

While much of the blame surely goes to the external forces, the role of parents cannot be ignored in spoiling the teenagers. Where were the parents when all these external influences were corrupting their kids? Who gave the car keys to the underage driver to go on a killer drive in the midnight? Who kept the revolver in the drawer or trained the kid to use it? Who gave the kid the most latest model cell phone as a loving present on his birthday? Who turned a blind eye on the kid returning home drunk from a rave party at 2 am? Who encourages pre-pubescent kids to perform obscene item numbers in the utterly vulgar reality shows? These are but only some of the teenage indulgences where parents need to be more responsible.

Handling Adult Children

"A child enters your home and for the next twenty years makes so much noise you can hardly stand it. The child departs, leaving the house so silent you think you are going mad," said author, John Andrew Holmes. But that is the way life is. Our roles and relationship change overtime. Once the children become grown up adults, we are no longer in a strictly parental role, spoon-feeding small, dependent, helpless children. They are matured, free, on their own and have their own little worlds to look after.

We need to treat our grown-up children as trusted friends. Be lovable but not authoritative. We should not unnecessarily exhort them. Do give your grown-ups advice if they ask for, but don't force your unsolicited opinions. Involve them in major decisions of the family. Support their decisions even if you do not fully agree with them. Practise a give-and-take relationship that's based on trust and companionship, and encourage them to do the same with you. Be generous to help them if they are in need and when appropriate be gracious to accept their offers of help.

We should always be positive and open to learning something new from our children. Let them instruct you, don't feel let down. Perhaps, they know better on current events and modern hi tech stuff than us. This attitude of learning from grown-up children helps narrow down the generation gap, which is a major cause of conflict in many families.

You may be lucky to live together with your children, but chances are that they would be living away from you in another city or country, because of job location. Or, they may be living in the same city, but not with you, because they want independence. There is nothing wrong in this. Let children enjoy the freedom and be happy in their own little family. In fact, in the present time the joint family system has broken down, leading the youngsters to stay away from their parents.

Traditions are almost always signs of growth, but they can bring feelings of loss. To get somewhere new, we may have to leave somewhere else behind. As children move out into the world, their parents can find themselves with mixed feelings. There are many parents who are attached to their children so much that they feel greatly depressed when the children leave them to live separately. At the time of writing this piece, I read the news of an air marshal (retired) committing suicide by shooting himself in his Chandigarh home in Punjab. As per his wife, both their children, married and employed, lived away from them – the son in Delhi and the daughter in Bangalore. Air marshal wanted his children to live with them in Chandigarh, but the children had their own preferences. He could not bear the separation from his children and went into the suicidal depression.

This is not an isolated case of parent's distress on account of living alone from children. Parents should learn to overcome unnecessary attachment with their adult children. Wise people call this attachment *moha,* and advise to shun it. Whether your children stay with you or independently, you should be happy either way. On your part, try to maintain good contacts with your children by personal visits, calling over phone, cyber chat, or any other means. Whenever possible spend more time with them.

Some parents have strained relations with their grown-up children. May be the children did not heed to the parents advice for choosing a career, a life partner, or a location to settle down. There may be many other occasions when children may take major decisions of life against the parents' wishes. The parents feel their children betrayed their love and concern for their good future. What should the parents do in such circumstances? Curse and frustrate themselves, swear relationship and disown the children, or respect their decisions and love them. Think over with a cool mind, and don't lose heart. Try to keep a good attitude by respecting their decisions they have taken. Surround them with love and goodness of God. No doubt, you advised them for their own benefit because of your genuine concern for their future, but they are grown up, and have the right of taking independent decisions. Let them decide their destiny. Remember: Each of our life journeys is unique. No child will take the same journey as the parent, and no parent can determine what a child's journey will be.

Grand Parenting

When your children were small, you were too busy building your career, working hard, perhaps doing overtime to earn more money for a nicer living, or travelling frequently away from home for business. You did not get enough time to cradle your infant, play fun games with your toddler, or help your school-going child in her home assignment. You missed all that fun and pleasure of being with the kids. And when you were somewhat settled and wanted to spend time with your kids, they have grown big, and love to be independent. They want the company of friends and peers, not you.

Grand parenting gives you the best opportunity to enjoy with your grandchildren. Being with young kids is a great pleasure. You too feel young in their company, and forget your worries. It's a great fun playing with the little ones, helping them learn new skills, leaving or receiving them at the school bus. Rahul Bajaj, the noted industrialist, now at 69 spends more time with his grandchildren and observes, "If I had known it was so fun, I would have had grand children before I had children." The other day we called our friends, Mrs. and Mr. Khokha in Jamnagar who had recently become grandparents. I asked them how they felt being *dada-dadi*. "Wonderful! I wish I had become *dadi* much before," said Mrs. Khokha.

Nana-nani and *dada-dadi's* bedtime stories are very famous. Your grandchildren would not sleep without you telling a story. What, if you run out of your stock of stories? You better read 'Chandamama', 'Vikram-Betal' or some other heroic and mythological tales to be handy. A scientist friend of mine, who never believed in mythology, read 'Ramayana', the great epic many times after his retirement, to pick up interesting tales for narration to his grandson. In the process, my friend, an atheist, became an ardent believer. Grandparents' interaction with children is not only a fun, but also an important platform for imbibing good habits and character building among the young ones. And in turn, the grandparents also learn new things.

If they are capable and willing, grandparents can help in the various household chores. For example, older generations have always assisted their children in childrearing. And with more married couples going to work, a healthier group of grandparents will have more opportunities in raising their grandchildren, and great-grandchildren, if they wish. In fact, in many families, grandparents are taking over the role of parents all over again by looking after the grandchildren, taking them to school, and attending to all their needs. A recent study in USA reveals that some 40 per cent grandparents who live near the young grandchildren are regularly providing childcare, while both the parents go to work.

There is always a generation gap between the elders and their children and grandchildren due to which a lot of misunderstanding and unhappiness is caused. What can one do to overcome this generation gap? While it is true that elders should correct the youngsters when they are wrong, what happens invariably is that older people tend to keep on preaching. They must realise that today's lifestyle is far different from theirs', and they should accept that. They should give more independence to both their children and the grandchildren. This way the youngsters will come to respect and love them more. More on generation gap in the next chapter.

6

Dealing with Your Parents

> By the time a man realises that may be his father was right, he usually has a son who thinks he's wrong.
>
> *Charles Wadsworth*

In the last chapter, we advised parents how to handle their children. Now it is your turn as children to know how to deal with your parents. We will spare small children from this responsibility and focus on the relationship of teenager and adult children with their parents.

You won't believe this chapter had been the most difficult for us to write. We were afraid our viewpoint on how grown-up children should deal with their parents would be labeled outdated and medieval. Perhaps, our advice would be ridiculed and rejected by children of the present generation, especially in the western world where most children leave home after age 16 or 17 to fend for themselves. They value freedom more than family ties and therefore prefer to lead their own independent lives right from a very young age. Even many parents in those cultures, who are concerned with their own independence, don't prefer their teenager and adult children to live with them.

Whereas mutual independence of parents and grown-up children may be a good way to satisfy the needs of both children and parents, a serious consequence of this independence can be seen in the increasing disharmony and stress in many family relationships. When away from parents, the grown-up children don't get the benefit of the experience and wisdom of parents to learn not to make the same mistakes their elders made. And the parents are deprived of the love and care of their children, especially when the parents grow older. So, where should one draw the line of mutual independence of grown-up children and parents? How the grown-up children should deal with their parents? This is the focus of the present chapter.

Coming to Terms

As a child, you looked to your parents for love, affection, approval, direction, security and support. Whether rich or poor, learned or ordinary, your parents tried to raise you in the best way they could at that time. Now, when you are grown up, you may question the way they reared you up. You may dislike some of the beliefs and traditions implanted in you by them. Many of you may harbour a few painful memories from your childhood, by how you were handled or treated by your parents. You may even feel hurt by some of the things they did to you. How would you deal with them? Do you want to repay the same to your parents or come to terms with any unresolved feelings and embrace your past with love and forgiveness?

No parent is an ideal parent. Whether you like it or not, and whether you are a parent yourself or not, the truth is that there is no perfection when it comes to parenting. There are no universities or colleges that give you degrees or diplomas in parenting. And there are no theories that teach how to be good parents. You learn it by experience, so did your parents while bringing you up, and probably you would also do the same when you become a parent yourself, if not already. "Before I got married I had six theories about bringing up children; now I have six children, and no theories," said British MP, John Wilmot.

Your childhood is a past now and you know you can't change it. But you can change the future by your right attitude to parenting. Now is the time to rid yourself of what did not go right and what you did not have while growing up. Give that to your children so that you do not repeat the same mistakes as you think your parents did.

Some grown-up children have strained relations with their parents. Perhaps, as a teenager son you did not listen to their advice while opting for a career. They wanted you to go for medicine, but you wanted to be a software engineer. Or, as your parents' darling daughter you married a young man they did not consider suitable for you. There may be several other occasions when grown-up children may take major decisions of life against their parents' wishes. What do you do in such circumstances? Curse and frustrate yourself, because you betrayed their love and concern for your better future. Disown them or swear relationship. Or respect their feelings and love them. Think over with a cool mind, and don't lose heart.

Although, they advised you for your benefit because of their genuine concern for your future, you are grown up, and have the right of taking independent decisions. But respect their feelings and concerns while you take major decisions of your life. Let these decisions not come in the way of your relationship with your parents.

Love and Respect Your Parents

In Hindu philosophy, there are seven *sukhas*, sources of happiness in one's life: *pitra sukha,* parental happiness; *santaana sukha*, offspring's happiness; *veevahika sukha,* marital happiness; *artha sukha*, material happiness; *swaasthya sukha*, health happiness; *vyavsahika sukha*, professional happiness and *aadhiatmica sukha*, spiritual happiness. The first three – parental happiness, offspring's happiness and marital happiness reflect our relationships in the family. As children, you are fortunate to experience *pitra sukha*, the happiness derived from the loving relationship with your parents. Are not those children unlucky who lost their parents early in life? They were deprived of the *pitra sukha* in their life.

Family, F-A-M-I-L-Y means father and mother I love you. Unless your parents were late bloomers, you would hopefully be grown up, be married, and have your own little world by now. Your welfare and happiness has a great reflection on the lives of your parents. If you are healthy, happily married and well settled in your career, you are a great source of strength and happiness to your parents. On the other hand there are many parents, who in spite of having all the comforts of life are leading very unhappy and frustrated lives, because their children have a broken marriage, unsuccessful career, or poor health. Do you know what most parents wish or ask in their prayer? "God let our children be happy and prosperous."

Be worthy of their prayers. Take efforts to live a healthy, happy, and fulfilling life. Love your mother and father, and put your heart and soul into making them happy as they did when you were small.

You may be lucky to live together with your parents, but chances are that you would be living away from them in another city or country, because of job location. Or, you may be living in the same city, but not with them, because you want independence. In fact, in the present times the joint family system has broken down, leading the youngsters to stay away from their parents. It's fine, you need to adjust with the changing times, but staying away from parents should not come in the way of your relationship with your parents.

If you are not staying with them, even then try to maintain good contacts with them by personal visits, calling over phone, cyber chat, or any other means. Let not only 'mothers' or 'fathers day' remind you of your parents. Remember them and whenever possible, visit them more often and spend more time with them. Most parents do not want anything from their grown-up children except their love and affection.

Whether you live with your parents or independently, you should respect them and seek their advice whenever required. Parents always think good of their children, and their advice will be in your benefit. There is a beautiful verse in Ramcharitmanas (Balkand, 76-2): *Matu-pita, guru prabhu ke bani, binai vichar karie shub jani*, which means the words of parents and guru are always good to be taken without any thinking.

Some grown-up children knowingly or unknowingly, undermine the importance or authority of elderly parents. The other day I saw an advertisement in the Wall Street Journal for auction of a house in Florida, U.S.A. The advertisement ran like this:

Enjoy this masterpiece setting on the Isleworth country club golf course, Florida with

- 8030+ Square Feet
- 5 Bedrooms
- 6 Baths
- 4 Car Garage
- Tropical Style Pool and Spa
- Guarded Security Gates
- Insulated Windows
- Tile Roofing
- Detached Mother-in-law Suite

Did you notice the place of the poor mother-in-law in the otherwise palatial home? A 'detached' suit! As if she is a maid and not part of the family. You are advised to give due importance to your parents and respect their authority or position in the family.

Being Grateful to Your Parents

Be grateful to your parents who brought you up with great love and blessings, often sacrificing their needs and enjoyments. In an interview to a national daily, Tina Ambani, wife of industrialist Anil Ambani said, "My mother-in-law Kokilaben is my idol. She is a fine example of ageing gracefully. Her charm and self-sufficiency show that redundancy does not set in with age. She constantly engages herself with causes she feels strongly about. I look up to her as my role model. A very important lesson that I learnt from her is that one has to make plans and start working on them. People will join you as you go along. The most important role that one can play is that of a catalyst to bring about a change."

There is a folk tale from Punjab that narrates how ungrateful and selfish some grown-up children could be to their parents: A young man was in love with a girl whom he wanted to marry. The girl was not so sure of his commitment to her and wanted to test him. She asked him that she would marry him only if he brings her the heart of his mother as a gift. He went home, stabbed his sleeping mother and took out her heart. As he was rushing to his girlfriend to present her the gift she wanted, he tumbled over. The mother's compassionate heart said, "Oh my son, hope you are all right. Be careful and don't get hurt."

As he reached his girlfriend and presented her his mother's heart, she said to him, "Go away, you mean fellow. When you could not be grateful to your own mother who did so much for you, how would you be loyal to me?"

There is a Jewish proverb that says, "God could not be everywhere and therefore he made mothers." Parents are great gifts of God. New Zealand's legendary TV host and journalist, Melanie Reid, pays rich tributes to mother, the God's gift in the following beautiful passage:

> My mother is a special gift,
> A special gift that God gave to me.
> I'd be lost and lonely without her,
> If God took her away you see.
> I love her so very much,
> That I couldn't bear to live without her healing touch.
> Thank you God for giving me such a loving mother.
> For I wouldn't want to be a part of any other

Another tribute to a mother from Simi Bajaj, which appeared in the Times of India on the occasion of Mother's day is also very inspiring.

> Her love is unconditional and pure
> Her presence sweet, soft and calm
> Her heart is full of deep emotions
> Her touch, like a soothing balm
> She is the anchor of wavering ships
> Sailing on the rough waters of life
> She slips with ease into the role of a mother
> After perfecting those of daughter and companion.

Our scripture are replete with stories of young people who gratefully made great sacrifices for their parents. Take for instance, Lord Rama, Shravana Kumar and Bhishama Pitamah who are the role models of ideal sons in our mythology. Rama went to jungles for fourteen years forsaking his coronation to carry out the orders of his father

Dashratha on the wish of his stepmother Kekaiye. Shravana Kumar carried his blind parents on his shoulders to fulfill their desire of going to various places of pilgrimage. And Bhishama Pitama vowed to remain unmarried throughout his life for the sake of his father who loved the same woman whom Bhishama was to marry.

To many, these stories may seem outdated mythological tales bearing no significance in the present times. But don't you hear of similar deeds of some children even today, who would do anything for the sake of their parents. Take for instance a recent case of terminally ill Suman Kapoor, a 54-year-old lawyer. He received a new lease of life after a successful liver re-transplant operation in Delhi's Sir Gangaram hospital. Do you know who donated the liver? His two sons- each donating half a liver for his father. It was the second liver transplant on him, a year-and-a-half after the first, in which also one of his two sons donated his half liver. Suman is now leading a normal life. This is all because of the sacrifices of his caring sons.

Bridging the Generation Gap

Although, there has always been and will be a generation gap between parents and the children, the technological age that we are now living in, has widened the gap drastically. Parents are generally unable to keep pace with the rapid advances in technology, which puts them out of gear with their children affecting relationships. The story below, which appeared in the year 2008 in *NY Times*, shows how technology like a cell phone has created a wide gap between parents and teenagers:

Russell Hampton, president of the Children's book and magazine publishing unit of Walt Disney Company was driving his teenage daughter Katie and her two friends to a play. Katie and her friends were sitting in the back seat talking to each other about some movie star. "I think it was Orlando Bloom," recalled Russell, whose company produced the movie 'Pirates of the Caribbean', in which the actor starred. "Oh dad, you are so out of it. We are talking of someone else," said Katie in a typical teenager sigh. After that the back-seat chat stopped. When Russell looked into his rear mirror he saw his daughter sending a text message on her cell phone, and he said to her, "Katie you should not be texting all the time. Your friends are there. It's rude." "But dad, we are texting each other. I don't want you to hear what I am saying."

Cars, homes, schools, malls, streets or other places, it is the same story. Children are increasingly using personal technological devices like cell phones, mini hand-held computers, social networking devices, pint-sized movie screens, instant messaging, and e-mail to define themselves and changing the way they communicate.

How can we bridge the generation gap? Here both children and parents have to play their parts. Parents should try to catch up with the technology. They should not hesitate to take help from their children who are more adept in the new technologies. There are host of modern gadgets and other home appliances, which children may know better how to handle than the parents. But that should be no reason for children to look down upon their parents because they (parents) are technologically outdated. They should instead help the parents to fill the technological gap that is the cause of many conflicts between generations.

We are in a new age, in which the younger generation has a new outlook. Their approach to life, people, and the environment is quite different from their parents. They don't simply accept many cultural, societal and family traditions and values. They see things more from scientific and practical angle than pure idealism. Children don't want to blindly follow the practices of their parents. That is fine. The grown-up children should be able to think in a new way, which can be different from their parents' ways. They need not be their parent's shadow. Parents should cherish their children for what they are, not for what you'd like them to be.

However, many times the problem with parents is that they want their children to be their carbon copies. They want their children to follow the traditions. Many times parents are too self-centered to pay careful attention to their children's 'radical' approach. As long as the younger generation honours the fundamental values of life – honesty, integrity, respect, compassion, empathy, humility, tolerance, trust, hard work, etc. the parents should give way to their children. Howsoever fashionable the values of the day, it is only the core moral values, handed down the generations that keeps society rooted on the right path. If parents and children are conscious of this fact, there will be much less conflict between generations.

Parents have certain strengths and so do the children. Whereas parents may have more maturity, wisdom and experience in life; innovation, entrepreneurship and vitality are the fortes of younger generation. Both should honour each other's strengths and overlook the weaknesses. This will bring synergy in the family and reduce the conflict of generations.

A friendly relationship between parents and grown-up children also helps to narrow the generation gap. Whereas most grown-up children want to see their parents as friends, parents are generally authoritarian and keep the boundaries. Be it a chat about their daughter's boyfriend, discussing some movie, or sharing a glass of beer with their teenage son, many parents of generation X have inhibitions and just want to be parents and not friends. Though it may be important to keep some boundaries between parents and children, parents can earn more love and understanding by being friends to their children. An open atmosphere of friendship also helps children to freely express their genuine problems to parents. The openness that comes with friendship is an advantage to both, but it can also result in an overly casual attitude towards parents. The extent to which the parents should be friendly with their children would vary from culture to culture.

Caring for Older Parents

Our roles and relationship change overtime. This is how an old parent puts his new role: "We have brought each other great love and blessings. In the past, your life was in my hands and that brought me joy. In the future, my life will be in your hands and that brings me peace." Everyone would become old one day that is the law of nature.

When parents are old they may need your loving care. Are you ready? Unfortunately many children of this generation are sadly neglecting the needs of their elderly parents. Our government has come up with new laws that make it compulsory for the children to take care of their elderly parents. But the fact is that as long as the children don't have the love and compassion for their old parents, no law can be helpful.

A young farmer toiled hard on his small field and earned barely enough to support a large family. His old father was too frail to do any work in the field or household. One day the son said to himself, "Of what use is this old man to me. I work hard under the scorching sun every day to make not even both ends meet for my dear children and wife, and this oldie only eats and sleeps the whole day. He is a burden to me, and I must get rid of him." So, he made a wooden crate, and let the old man lie down in it. Then he covered the crate and carried it on a wheelbarrow to the top of the cliff near by. As he was about to throw the crate downhill, he heard a feeble voice from inside the crate. He opened it, and listened to his father saying, "Son, why are you wasting the container. Take me out and throw me down. Save the container for future, as your son will need it anyway."

As parents grow older, they may need certain aids or gadgets – hearing aids, dentures, glasses, walking sticks, magnifying lenses, bigger prints, and fonts to improve their living. Be generous to help them if they are in need. How some children are indifferent to the genuine needs of their elderly parents is beautifully portrayed in the Indian movie 'Baghban' in which Amitabh Bachhan and Hema Malini play the role of parents.

They raised four sons to the best of their means, even spending much of their retirement savings. So, when Amitabh retires as a bank manager, he receives paltry pension benefits not enough to be self-reliant. The sons who were eyeing on the hefty share of the father's wealth were disappointed when they learnt that they have to support their elderly parents.

Reluctantly, the four sons agreed to keep one parent at a time in turns. During the turn of his stay with the eldest son, one day Amitabh broke his spectacles. He hesitantly asked his son to get him a new pair of glasses so that he could read the letter received from the mother who was staying with the second son in another city. The son and his wife said, "Papa, wait till the next month as we have lots of other expenses this month." Helpless, Amitabh keeps quiet.

The next day, their seven-year-old son Rinku wanted a new school uniform and the parents gladly said they would buy him the same in the evening. The child who had heard the previous day's dialogue between his parents and the grandfather said innocently, "Daddy, but why don't you buy the spectacles for grandpa first. He has not read to me two letters from grandma?" Alas, daddy could realise his responsibility to his daddy!

Not all the grown-up children are like those illustrated above. Sometimes, though the children may be very sensitive to the needs of their old parents, the difficulties come from the parents themselves to receive any help. Although old age may have crept on them, some aging parents just won't accept that they can't do certain things by themselves and might need some assistance in doing their day-to-day tasks. "I am not that old to use a stick or dentures" type seniors may reject any assistance. Some elderly parents may be adamant to receive any sort of medication, though their medical condition may warrant it. This attitude of rejection largely comes from pride that keeps elderly people from accepting the changes and challenges of old age.

Some elderly parents may also acquire a form of self-denial over the changes that are happening to them. This may be due to debilitating illness or condition, which causes drastic changes in the elders' lifestyle. In such cases, care for older parents can be a very difficult task.

Rejection or self-denial is actually a common problem in caring for aging parents. You need to be thoughtful and considerate.

Old age is another childhood and some elders do behave like small children – stubborn, adamant. Handle them patiently and provide what they need to improve the quality of their life. Remember your childhood! Your parents did all the possible tricks and excuses to persuade you to drink milk, eat, play, bathe or sleep. Perhaps, it is now your turn to do the same to your older parents.

This reminds me of an old dad and mom's letter in which they write to their son and daughter to be patient and considerate to them. The letter goes like this:

Dear son, dear daughter,

The day you find that I have become very old, try to have some patience with me and try to understand me.

If I get dirty while eating, if I have some difficulty dressing, be patient and remember the hours that I spent teaching you these things when you were small.

If I repeat the same thing dozens of time, do not interrupt me. Listen to me. When you were small, you kept asking me to read you the same story, evening after evening, until you fell asleep. And I did it happily!

If I don't wash myself so often under the shower, do not be angry and tell me that it is shame. Remember, how many excuses I had to invent to make you take a bath when you were small.

By seeing my ignorance of new technologies don't laugh at me but give me time to understand. Remember, I taught you so many things – to eat well, to dress well, to behave well, and how to confront the problems of the life.

When my poor legs will not allow me to move as before, help me in the same way as when I held your hands to teach you take your first steps.

If I sometimes lose memory or am not able to follow a conversation, give me the necessary time to recollect and if I do not get there, don't become a nervous and arrogant person because the most important thing for me is to be with you and be able to speak to you.

If I refuse to eat, don't force me! I know very well when I am hungry and when I am not hungry.

And when one day, I shall say to you that I don't want to live any more, that I want to die, don't get angry, because one day you will also understand. Try to understand that at certain age, we do not really live any more. We simply survive!

You don't have to feel sad, unfortunate or incompetent in front of my old age and of my state. You have to understand what I live for.

One day, you will understand that in spite of all my errors, I always wanted what was best for you.

Help me to walk, help me to end my life with love and patience. The only thing that I need from you is a smile and a lot of love.

I love you my son, my daughter!

Your dad, your mom

Eyeing on Parent's Property

Some children may be lucky to inherit a lot of wealth from their parents. Although, in India and many other countries children are the natural inheritors of their parents' property, grown-up children will not do any good by always keeping an eye on the wealth of their parents. The lure or hope of getting a fortune from the parents keeps many children away from hard work and self-reliance. Such children are waiting for the free wealth to come to them without putting any efforts. Sometimes, if children have unlimited access to parents wealth, they may even fritter it away, and in the end be paupers. Children should be able to live on their own earnings and not look at the riches of their parents. If you want to achieve something high in life, do not unnecessarily worry about the natural inheritance, which will happen anyway. Instead, focus on your chosen goal in life and toil hard to achieve it.

Disputes over inheritance of parents' property have been a major cause of strained relations in many families. For all their lives the parents sweat hard and when the time to enjoy the wealth comes, the children may forcefully demand their right. Serious rift between parents and their children or among children and other relations have cropped up over inheritance of property. There have been many instances where grown-up children have even murdered their parents or siblings over property matters. This is really very shameful.

In many western countries, children do not have any natural right over the wealth of their parents. Right to property is according to what is willed by the parents and not a natural transfer. That is a social tradition and also the law in these counties. Many people in these countries will their wealth away to public institutions such as hospital, colleges, schools, research institutes, libraries and NGOs etc. Perhaps, making a will is a better system than the natural inheritance of parents' assets, which will result in cordial relationship between parents and their grown-up children.

7

Friends are a Treasure to Keep

> Best friends are like diamonds,
> precious and rare.
> False friends are like leaves,
> found everywhere.
>
> *Anonymous*

There's a miracle called friendship, which offers relationship of a lifetime. One does not know how it happens or when it gets started, but we know the special joy it brings when it happens. Friendship is a wonderful relationship that brings people of different castes and creeds, people of different cultures, people of different nations, people of different faiths, and people rich and poor, together.

Few relations in earth never die. Yes, that is what the word 'FRIEND' stands for – F is for few, R for relations, I for in, E for earth, N for never, and D for die. Friends are very rare jewels to have. They walk in to help you when the rest of the world walks out. They love you, make you smile, and encourage you to succeed. They listen to you, they praise you, and they are a big source of strength. Friends, indeed, are God's most precious gift to us.

"And what is friendship? It is the hardest thing in the world to explain. "It is not something you learn in school. But if you have not learned the meaning of friendship, you really have not learned anything at all," said Mohammad Ali, theologian and former vice president of Iran. Yes, friendship can't be taught, it is to be nurtured and experienced. How? Here are some guidelines, which may not only inspire you to understand the meaning of true friends, but also make you one.

Who is a True Friend?

Every day, we greet with a wave and smile, so many people – shoppers in the mall, people in the street, travelers in the plane, train or bus, colleagues at work, fishing or tennis buddies, people in the temple, and elsewhere. Do we call them all true friends? Some people come into our lives and quickly go, some stay for a while and leave such an impression on our heart and soul that we are changed forever. They are, indeed, the true, faithful friends, the rest are mere acquaintances.

A true friend is described very beautifully in verses 6.2 - 4 of *Kishkindakand* in Goswami Tulsidas' *Ramcharitamanas*. In these verses, Shri Ram explains the *dharma* of a true friend to the monkey king Sugreeva, while befriending him: One who saves his friend from the wrong path, and leads him on the right. A true friend highlights his friend's virtues, but hides his faults; does not doubt his friend in dealings. He always does well to his friend, and loves him hundred times more in case of adversity. Shri Ram adds further that a friend who speaks good on your face but speaks ill at the back; one whose heart is impure and crooked like the gait of a snake, should always be forsaken.

Digha Nikaya, the famous Buddhist Scripture also gives a similar explanation of a true friend. It says:

> The friend who always seeks his benefit,
>
> The friend whose words are other than his deeds,
>
> The friend who flatters just to make you pleased.
>
> The friend who keeps you company in wrong,
>
> These are four the wise regard as enemies;
>
> Shun them from afar as paths of danger.
>
> The friend who is a helper all the time,
>
> The friend in happiness and sorrow both,
>
> The friend who gives advice that's always good.
>
> These the wise see as good-hearted friends
>
> And with devotion cherish such as these
>
> As does a mother cherish her own child....

"Who finds a faithful friend, finds a treasure," is a Jews saying. True friends are like diamonds, precious and rare. Anything lesser than that is not worth having a friend. "Associate yourself with men of good quality if you esteem your own reputation; for 'tis better to be alone than in bad company," advised George Washington.

Time and again wise men have advised to keep company with good friends. How the company of a good friend fortifies you and that of an evil friend harms you, is very beautifully explained in verse 57b of the *Balkanda* of *Ramcharitmanas* which reads as: *Jalu pey saris bikai, dekhyu preeti ki reeti bhali. Bilag hoi rasu jaai, kapatt khatai parat puni.* The verse says; see the beauty of water's friendship with milk! In association with milk, the water also sells at the price of milk. But the same milk splits when it has the company of sour.

You may have many friends, but true, quality friends whom you can trust may be very few. Most friends hang around only for selfish motives, and vanish when really needed. Do you remember the story of the two friends and the bear? How quickly the friend who was boasting of his friendship and vowing to keep company of the other, climbed on the tree as he saw a bear approaching them. Who is a true friend? "A true friend is the person who steps in when the whole world steps out," a sage said.

Fortunate are those who have such friends. It is said that a true friend is hard to find, hard to lose, and impossible to forget. Where do you find such friends? They may be among your old schoolmates; colleagues; religious, cultural or social group members; or your neighbours. In fact, your neighbours can be your best friends, dependable, helpful and handy. That is why the Bible says: Love thy neighbor as thyself.

"Your neighbour is your other self dwelling behind a wall. In understanding, all walls shall fall down. Who knows but that your neighbour is your better self, wearing another body? See that you love him as you would love yourself," said philosopher, poet Kahlil Gibran in his work *Jesus, The Son of Man.*

Some people, however, have difficulty making friends with their neighbours. They can talk to people on cell phone at distant places, and chat with people at the remotest corner of the globe on the Internet, but have difficulty talking to their neighbour next door. Man has been all the way to the moon and back, and is now trying for the Mars, but has trouble in crossing the street to meet the new neighbour. How paradoxical! "I have lost friends, some by death, others through sheer inability to cross the road," said

Virginia Woolf, twentieth century English Novelist and essayist.

Unfortunately many people do not have good friends. Either because they are so busy in their profession, they neglect friends in favour of their careers. Or they look for the perfect friend, which they never find. "One who looks for a friend without faults will have none' goes a Hasidic saying. And some people are so caught up in who's right and who's wrong among friends that they forget what's right and wrong. Sometimes we just don't realise what real friendship means until it is too late. Remember, friends are like balloons; once you let them go, you might not get them back. But often, we get so busy with our own lives and problems that we may not even notice that we've let them fly away.

Be Worthy of Your Friends

Let us learn the virtues of a true friend from the above scriptural sayings, and make us worthy of our friends. The following lines of Frank Dempster, the famous American graphics professor and writer in which he prays God for making him worthy of his friends, are very inspiring.

> It is my joy in life to find,
> At every turning of the road,
> The strong arm of a comrade kind,
> To help me onward with my load,
> And since I have no gold to give,
> And love alone must make amend,
> My only prayer is, while I live –
> God make me worthy of my friends.

Remember: we are human magnets that like attracts like, and that what we give, we get. Therefore the first step to having good friends is to be a good friend yourself. "The only way to have a friend is to be one," said Ralph Waldo Emerson, the noted American philosopher.

Like other relationships, friendship is also based on love for one another. In Persian, the verb, 'to love' means 'to befriend'. So, the expression 'I love you' literally means 'I have you as a friend'. Love your friends honestly, and let them know that you care for them. Verbalise your feeling of love for your friends.

Did you notice the world 'honestly'? Yes, in friendship 'honesty' is the key word. Whatever the situation, one should always be honest to his or her friends. Praise them honestly and openly whenever, wherever required. Say honestly you're sorry, when you hurt your friends. Don't let them assume it.

Two friends, a boy and a girl were playing together. The boy had a collection of marbles.

The girl had some sweets with her. The boy told the girl that he will give her all his marbles in exchange for her sweets. The girl agreed. The boy kept the biggest and the most beautiful marble aside and gave the rest to the girl. The girl gave him all her sweets as she had promised. That night, the girl slept peacefully. But the boy couldn't sleep as he kept wondering if the girl had hidden some sweets from him the way he had hidden his best marble.

Moral of the story: If you don't give your hundred per cent in a relationship, you'll always keep doubting if the other person has given his or her hundred per cent. This is applicable for any relationship may that be a friend, husband, wife, employer, employee, etc. Give your hundred per cent to everything you do and be happy!

One should get rid of hypocrisy, artificiality and pretence, as these are the obstacles to true friendship. Be simple and humble. When two people are friends, they can speak openly to each other. If they don't like something or have different opinion, they can say that to the other person without any fear or hesitation. Quietly disagreeing is normal, but noisy 'no's make enemies. In a friendship, the relationship is sustained, despite differences of views. True friends are sympathetic of each other's faults. If you are a good friend, you should close your eyes to the faults of your friends, and open them to your own.

To be a good friend you should have an understanding heart and a forgiving nature. Have trust in your friends, and share your moments of happiness and sorrow with them with open heart. "You can't shake hands with a clenched fist," said Indira Gandhi.

Equality in Friendship

Friendship can exist only when there is a feeling of equality towards each other. "You cannot be friends upon any other terms than upon the terms of equality," said Woodrow Wilson. Do not confuse equality among friends in terms of financial status, position or power. These things are not important in true friendship. And even if they were important, it is difficult to find two friends who are equal in all respects. Both may be equally wealthy, but may not be occupying equal positions or status in society or profession. Or they may be equally reputed in society, but one may have a lot of money while the other may be a humble social worker. Further, two friends may be equal in wealth and status, but may have different colour, creed, culture or nationality. So, it is very difficult to find two friends who are equal in all respects. In fact, it is the feeling of equality and respect for your friend that matters, and not the riches, power, colour or creed.

There are numerous examples of friends – one being very rich and the other poor, or one occupying a high office or position in society and the other being an ordinary person. Have you heard of the friendship of Lord Krishna and the poor Sudama as told in the Mahabharta?

Krishna was the king of Dwarka and Sudama was a poor Brahmin. Both were best friends from their school days. If Sudama desired, Lord Krishna would have made him a billionaire or a minister, but both never wanted money or position to come in the way of their friendship. They were happy as friends. As the tale goes, one day,

Sudama's wife coerced her husband to go to Dwarka to seek Krishna's help, as she could no longer bear the pains of poverty. "Oh God, why did you make us so poor. We live in a thatched hut, don't make both ends meet and can't even send our children to school. What a curse!" she complained and said, "You always say your friend, Krishna is a king, so why don't you go to him and ask for some help?"

Reluctantly, Sudama left for Dwarka. Weird, sad and clad in rags, he reached the kingdom of Dwarka after a three day's long, tiresome journey on foot. But, the guards won't allow him to enter the palace. When he said that he was the friend of Krishna, the guards laughed and said, "No, our king does not have any beggar as his friend." When he pleaded that Krishna was indeed his best friend from the school days, the guards informed the King. And Lo! Krishna came running with open arms and embraced his friend. Meeting after a long time, they hugged each other with immense joy and ecstasy.

Sudama was overwhelmed with royal treatment given to him by his friend Krishna, his wives and the subjects. Nostalgia of the school days overtook both the friends, and they talked about their lives. True to his friendship, Sudama did not express his poor plight and to ask for help, but Krishna understood his friend's misfortune. After a week's sojourn amid the splendor of his friend's kingdom, Sudama took leave of his friend. On reaching his village, Sudama was amazed to see the riches and grandeur of his family. His eyes could not believe it, but his heart conveyed everything.

Wealth, position, power, fame or name does not matter in true friendship. It is the feeling of true love between the friends that matters. "The most I can do for my friend is simply to be his friend. I have no wealth to bestow on him. If he knows that I am happy in loving him he will want no other reward. Is not friendship divine in this?" said Henry David Thoreau, the nineteenth century American poet, philosopher and naturalist.

You Can't Have Too Many Friends

"True friendship consists not in multitude of friends, but in their worth and value," said Ben Johnson, Hollywood actor and stuntman. It is better to have a handful of quality friends that you can trust and open your heart to, instead of maintaining a large inventory of friends who just flock around for selfish motives, and would go away on small pretext. "Books, like friends, should be few and well chosen," said Samuel Paterson. Have you heard the story of a hare that had many friends but none came to her help when she was in need?

A hare was very popular with the other animals in the jungle that all claimed to be her friends. One day she heard the hounds approaching her and hoped to escape them by the aid of her friends. So, she went to the horse, and asked him to carry her away from the hounds on his back. But he declined, stating that he had important work to do for his master. "He felt sure," he said, "that all her other friends would come to her assistance." She then applied to the bull, and hoped that he would repel the hounds with his horns. The bull replied: "I am very sorry, but I have an appointment with a lady; but I feel sure that our friend, the goat will do what you want." The goat, however, feared that his back might do her some harm if he took her upon it. The ram, he felt sure, was the proper friend to ask for help. So she went to the ram and told him the case. The ram replied: "Another time, my dear friend. I do not like to interfere on the present occasion, as hounds have been known to eat sheep as well as hares." The hare then went, as a last hope, to the calf who regretted that he was unable to help her, as he did not like to take the responsibility upon himself, as so many older persons than he had declined the task. By this time the hounds were quite near, and the hare took to her heels and luckily escaped.

This tale is not real but gives a beautiful moral that says: He that has many friends has no friends. You can't have too many friends because then you are just not really friends. Further, as we grow, the number of friends keeps growing bigger, and unless we constantly renew the list of our friends, it is difficult to maintain a worthwhile relationship with all. If a man does not make new acquaintance as he advances through life, he will soon find himself left alone. "A man, Sir, should keep his friendship in constant repair," said Samuel Johnson, British lexicographer.

Of course, it is hard to forget true friends. They are mutual bonds for life that can't be given up. A true friend is like a computer. He comes to 'enter' in your life, 'save' you in his heart, 'format' your problems, 'shift' you to opportunities, and never 'delete' you from his 'memory'!

Be Supportive of Your Friends

You must sincerely appreciate the contributions your friends make in your life. Be grateful, and convey your thanks even for the small things your friends do for you.

Your friend may have dreams, everyone has. A good friend is always sensitive and responsive to the needs, dreams, and goals of his friends. Encourage your friends to realise their dreams and aspirations. Pray and wish them good luck in their endeavours. Cheer them. We all need encouragement now and then and when it comes from friends its effect is magical. "Whenever a friend succeeds, a little something in me dies," said Gore Vidal, the contemporary American, novelist and screenwriter.

Unfortunately there are some friends who are jealous of their buddies. They envy their friends' success. That is why probably Oscar Wilde, the famous Irish poet and playwright said: "Anybody can sympathise with the sufferings of a friend, but it requires a very fine nature to sympathise with a friend's success."

I myself have experienced the truth contained in the above quote of Oscar Wilde. I often talk about my amateur writing with friends, and seek their opinions through e-mails or in person whenever I get to meet them in parties or other occasions. Most friends encourage my writing and even give valuable suggestions for improvement. However, one of my close friends and onetime colleague (Mr. X) always showed his indifference whenever I talked about some topic of a book I would have been working on.

One day, when I presented the copy of my newly published book, *Retired but not Tired* to some friends in a party, they all were so happy that they gave me a big applause. They turned on the pages of the book with lot of interest to see what was there inside. I was overwhelmed with joy. However, I noticed that Mr. X was not happy. In fact, he seemed so upset that he did not even look at the book and kept it aside frowningly. Though I had known of his apathy to my writing on many occasions, but never realised he could be so jealous of my success in my newfound pastime of writing books.

A fable tells that two friends were walking through the desert. During some point of the journey they had an argument, and one friend slapped the other one in the face. The one who got slapped was hurt, but without saying anything, wrote in the sand: "Today my best friend slapped me in the face."

They kept on walking until they found an oasis, where they decided to take a bath. The one, who had been slapped, got stuck in the mire and started drowning, but the friend saved him. After the friend recovered from near drowning, he wrote on a stone: "Today my best friend saved my life."

The friend who had slapped and saved his best friend asked him, "After I hurt you, you wrote in the sand and now, you write on a stone, why?"

The other friend replied: "When someone hurts us, we should write it down in sand where winds of forgiveness can erase it away. But, when someone does something good for us, we must engrave it in stone where no wind can ever erase it."

Sacrificing for Friends

Sam and Jason, the two inseparable friends met with an accident on their way to Boston City. The following morning, Jason woke up blind and Sam was still unconscious. Dr. Berkeley was standing at his bedside looking at his health chart and medications with a thoughtful expression on his face. When he saw Sam awake, he beamed at him and asked, "How are you feeling today Sam?" Sam tried to put up a brave face and smiled back saying, "Absolutely wonderful Doctor. I am very grateful for all that you have done for me." Dr Berkeley was moved at Sam's deed. All that he could say was, "You are a very brave man Sam, and God will make it up to you in one way or another". While he was moving on to the next patient, Sam called back at him almost pleading, "Promise me you won't tell Jason anything."

"You know I won't do that. Trust me." and walked away. "Thank you," whispered Sam. He smiled and looked up in prayer. "I hope I live up to your ideas...please give me the strength to be able to go through this... Amen."

Months later when Jason had recuperated considerably, he stopped hanging around with Sam. He felt discouraged and embarrassed to spend time with a disabled person like Sam.

Sam was lonely and disheartened, since he didn't have any body else other than Jason to count on. Things went from bad to worse. And one day Sam died in despair. When Jason was called on his burial, he found a letter waiting for him. Dr Berkeley gave it to him with an expressionless face and said, "This is for you Jason. Sam had asked me to give it to you when he was gone".

In the letter he had said: "Dear Jason, I have kept my promise in the end to lend you my eyes if anything had happened to them. Now there is nothing more that I can ask from God, than the fact that you will see the world through my eyes. You will always be my best friend...Sam." When he had finished reading Dr. Berkeley said, "I had promised Sam to keep his sacrifice he made a secret from you. But now I wish I didn't stick it because I don't think it was worthy of it".

All that was left for Jason while he stood there was tears of regret and memories of Sam for the rest of his life.

Lesson of the story: No matter who we make a friend, we should stick by him till the end. Life is really meaningless without a friend. This story may be an extreme act of sacrifice for a friend. Everybody may not do that, but one can certainly offer help to a needy friend in many other ways. 'A friend in need is a friend indeed', is an old adage. Be there when your friends need you or you may wind up alone. Really listen; a friendly ear is a soothing balm. Offer to help, and also know when to say 'no thanks'. Examine your motives before you 'help' out. "I might give my life for my friend, but he had better not ask me to do up a parcel," said Logan Pearsall Smith, noted American writer and essayist.

Friends and Money Matters

Money has been the root cause of failure of many friendly relationships. Be cautious about lending money to friends. You might lose both. Money might make you wealthy, but friends make you rich. "The holy passion of friendship is so sweet and steady and loyal and enduring in nature that it will last through a whole lifetime, if not asked to lend money," said Mark Twain.

"A friendship founded on business is better than a business founded on friendship," said John D. Rockefeller. A friend sent me the following e-mail that I would like to share with you:

> Money, Money, Money
> It can buy a House
> But not a Home

Friends are a Treasure to Keep   133

It can buy a Bed
But not Sleep
It can buy a Clock
But not Time
It can buy you a Book
But not Knowledge
It can buy you a Position
But not Respect
It can buy you Medicine
But not Health
It can buy you Blood
But not Life

So, you see, Money isn't everything. And it often causes pain and suffering. I tell you all this because I am your Friend, and as your Friend I want to take away your pain and suffering. So send me all your money and I will suffer for you."

From: A true friend you will never find

Life is Fun with Friends

Enjoy with your friends. Always remember that friendship is worth it when you are able to enjoy the amazing relationship with no holds barred. It is not what we call a friendship if you don't feel right. Get together with friends often, and talk frequently. You are lucky if your friends live nearby and you can meet them

frequently. You can form a small group of friends who meet regularly. For instance we have a kitty party of seven couples. We get together in one another's house by rotation every month. The half-day session is full of enjoyment with tambola, yoga, some party games, chitchat, lunch and evening tea. We have another group of friends who are part of our *Sunderland* club. Here also, we meet once in a month in someone's house in rotation. It is a four-hour programme of reciting *Sunderkhand,* chanting *kirtan* and having lunch together. Everyone looks forward to the next get-together in both the groups.

If your friends are not located nearby and you are not able to meet them more often, try to be in touch with them through telephone, letters, e-mail or whatever. Communication is an important factor in any relationship, and friendship is no exception. Friends may be out of sight, but should not be out of mind. Madhu and Vijay are our good friends living in Mumbai. They have made it a habit to check their diary every morning and see which of their 200 friends and relatives around the world have birthday or wedding anniversary. They will invariably call or e-mail and wish the friend on the occasion. And what a great pleasure for the recipient friend!

Om and Laji Kakar are our very old friends. We lived in the same neighbourhood in Delhi for about ten years. Our and Kakar's children were of the similar ages and were also good friends. It was great fun visiting each other often, partying, sharing meals and celebrating festivals together. On *Karvachhauth,* a festival when wives keep a whole day fast for the welfare of their husbands, we would call each other to tell the sighting of the moon so that the ladies could end their fast. We have maintained this communication for the last thirty years even when we had been away in America. Though the timing of moonrise was different in India and America, we would call each other on phone to announce the sighting of the moon.

For friends living far from you, especially in countries in different time zones, one of the most convenient and economical ways to be in touch with them is through e-mail. I myself have about 300 e-mail addresses – some close friends, and others, professional acquaintances. I am in regular touch with most friends via e-mail – sending them greetings on the New Year and other festivals, wishing happy birthdays, wedding anniversaries, giving yoga consultations, exchanging notes on issues of common interest, and soliciting their views on my books and articles.

I never used e-mail so extensively before. Now, it is my main method of communication to stay connected with friends and relations. I believe the Internet will play an increasingly important role in connecting ourselves with friends and relatives living at distant locations, especially because of different time zones or when our movement is restricted because of old age, or some disabling disease.

Have you ever realised that retirement could actually be great fun with friends? Experience the joy of life in retirement with your best friends. Imagine travelling together to distant places; chilling out at a beach; having a morning yoga session, or a long evening walk together; playing tennis, cards and chess; or catching up with old times. No responsibilities, no hassles, and a lot of like-minded interests and hobbies to share. I fondly cherish the four trips - Shimla, Manali, Vaishnudevi, and Haridwar - that we made with some of our friends soon after our retirement. For the first time, I truly enjoyed travelling. No worries of the office - leftover jobs, emergency calls, or reporting back! No limitation of time and space! I remember the phrase 'we are in no hurry' during our trip to Haridwar in 2002. We were two freshly retired couples and used this phrase jokingly so often while driving, halting at wayside eateries, bathing long hours in the holy Ganges, shopping, and listening to discourses in various ashrams. We were in no hurry indeed. We savoured every moment of the trip, and the pleasure was doubled because we had friends to share with.

Friendship Day

Perhaps, you know that first Sunday of August every year is celebrated as the International Friendship Day. It is a time to recognize your friends and the contribution they make to your life. Although the tradition of dedicating this day in honour of friends began in USA in 1935, the practice gradually gained popularity in many countries of the world. On this day people spend time with their friends and express love for them by exchanging friendship gifts like flowers, cards and wristbands, etc.

Should friendship be just a one-day affair in a year? No, friendship is forever, and it is a pretty full-time occupation if you are truly friendly with somebody. However, caught between the pressures of the modern times, we may lose track of our friends, and the Friendship day is a good reminder to remember, recognise and honour our friends. So, celebrate the Friendship Day every year with great spirits, and let the memories of true friendship reverberate in your life throughout the year.

Last year on the Friendship day, I sent an e-mail message to many friends. In response I received some beautiful and inspiring messages, poems and quotes on friendship, which I compiled together along with several others that I picked up from a few websites. Following are those messages, quotes and poems that not only make us understand the meaning of true friendship but also inspire us to become a better friend.

> Stars have five ends, squares have four ends, triangles have three ends, lines have two ends, life has one end, but I hope friendship has no ends.
>
> *Praveen*

A single candle can illuminate an entire room. A true friend lights up an entire lifetime. Thanks for the bright light of your friendship.

Mahesh

Don't walk in front of me, I may not follow; don't walk behind me, I may not lead. Walk beside me and be my friend.

Albert Camus

True friends will not have any reason for their friendship. So it can never be broken when they don't find that reason.

Kumarswamy

Good friends are like stars – you don't always see them, but you know they are always there.

A friend scolds like a dad, cares like a mom, teases like a sister, irritates like a brother. Friendship is the blend of all relations.

Sri

Rahi badal jate hai par raste nahi badalte,
Toofan aaye fir bhi mausam nahi badalte,
Gile shikaive bhale kitane ho,
Magar sacche dost kabhi nahin badalte.

Sweetu

Only your real friends will tell you when your face is dirty.

Sicilian Proverb

What is a friend? A single soul dwelling in two bodies.

Aristotle

A true friend is someone who thinks that you are a good egg even though he knows that you are slightly cracked.

Bernard Meltzer

When we honestly ask ourselves which person in our lives mean the most to us, we often find that it is those who, instead of giving advice, solutions, or cures, have chosen rather to share our pain and touch our wounds with a warm and tender hand.

Samuel Paterson

A single rose can be my garden...a single friend, my world.

Leo Buscaglia

A true friend is one who overlooks your failures and tolerates your success.

Doug Larsen

Friendship is the only cement that will ever hold the world together.

Woodrow Wilson

Friendship without self-interest is one of the rare and beautiful things of life.

James Francis Byrnes

Friendship is always a sweet responsibility, never an opportunity.

Kahlil Gibran

A true friend is the most precious of all possessions and the one we take the least thought about acquiring.

La Rochefoucauld

Friends are God's way of taking care of us.

Marlene Dietrick

There is magic in the memory of schoolboy friendships; it softens the heart and even affects the nervous system of those who have no heart.

Benjamin Disraeli

A true friend is some one you can trust with all your secrets.

Anonymous

Money may make you wealthy, but friends make you rich.

Anonymous

> A friend is someone who reaches for your hand, but touches your heart.
>
> *Kathleen Grove*

> In the end, we will remember not the words of our enemies, but the silence of our friends.
>
> *Martin Luther King Jr.*

Your Extended Relationships

Taking a broader perspective, your relationships extend beyond your wife, children, and close relations or friends. The Indian philosophy believes in *'Atmvat sarvbhuteshu'*, *'Vasudev Katumbkam'*, *'Serve bhuvantu sukhino'* meaning, the whole world is your family. According to this philosophy, every human being is part of the all-pervading Divine Mother who is the originator of the entire creation. We are all 'Her' children, and therefore form an extended family. Unfortunately, the spirit of universal brotherhood is strongly lacking among people in modern times. Perhaps, that is the main cause of so much tension, conflict, hatred, and jealousy all over the world. Each one is at the other's throat to corner more wealth for oneself. He is out to get ahead of others in the mad race for material comforts and luxuries. People or the nations, it is the same story everywhere. "Either men will learn to live like brothers, or they will die like beasts," said Max Lerner.

> A relationship doesn't shine by just shaking hands in good times. But it blossoms by holding firmly in critical times.

Let everyone, young and old, imbibe the spirit of extended family, and live as good brothers and sisters. Only then can there be peace and love in this world. Extend your love and compassion beyond your close and dear ones. Embrace the larger community as your family. We tend to come together when there is disaster - earthquake, flood, cyclone or others. How about coming together to prevent disaster? The seniors, because of their experience and maturity, can serve as a catalyst in inspiring others to imbibe the spirit of universal brotherhood, and play an important role in promoting love and peace in society. They should spare some time and involve themselves in community welfare activities. There are so many social organizations that are working in promoting peace and friendship among people of the world. Find out how you can give your share in making this world a little better place.

8

Relationships at Workplace

> Work is love made visible. And if you cannot work with love but only with distaste, it is better that you should leave your work and sit at the gate of the temple and take alms of those who work with joy.
>
> *Kahlil Gibran*

Relationships at workplace! For those who have no regard for labour and look for their self-interest only, the concept of relationships at workplace may seem absurd. However, the need of having good relationships at one's workplace is no less important than that in any other relationship. With almost one-third of our life spent at the workplace, or perhaps even more with the extended work hours in the present-day highly demanding world, workplace is virtually where we live. We interact with our seniors, peers, and subordinates in-house, and numerous customers outside. How we relate and interact with them has not only a great bearing on our personal performance and that of the company we work for, but also on our overall life.

A workplace is not where you hire some people to turn out products and services to best serve only the owners' interests, and fire them on any pretext when those interests are at stake. In fact, an ideal workplace is an institution or organization where people – owners, managers and subordinates come together to work for the mutual benefit of society serving everyone's interests. "Coming together is a beginning; keeping together is progress; working together is success," said someone. The words 'company' or 'corporation' for the workplace reflect this concept of togetherness and cooperation of people who work in them. Good companies not only make profits, they also care to nourish and nurture their people and the communities around them.

An organization is nothing without its people, they are the ones who add value and make a difference. No amount of technological improvement, financial back up or marketing strategy can make an organization excellent unless it has healthy, happy, and creative people. But today's fast paced, stressful life, insecurity, tough competition, and globalization is making people victim of serious physical, psychological, and emotional disorders that adversely affect their relationships and life at work, home and elsewhere.

Time and again, companies have faced the problem of human relations - how to deal with people. How to keep people healthy, happy and creative so that they perform at their peak, is a big corporate challenge today. In a world where relationships matter more than ever, human relations, skills or abilities at the workplace matter the most. "The ability to deal with people is as purchasable a commodity as sugar or coffee. And I will pay more for that ability than for any other under the sun," said John D. Rockefeller.

Workplace is a Family

Our work has a great influence on our lives. It occupies a large part of our day, it is our identity, our main source of social standing, and it affects our health physically, mentally and emotionally. People generally associate us with what we do. In fact, the workplace is to a great extent our big family where we live. It is a corporate family where every member – the employers and the employees - shares a common vision and gets equal opportunity to fulfill his or her needs. A healthy workplace should provide ample opportunities to all its members to grow and accomplish their missions, and share the happiness and sorrow associated with it. How would such a workplace be? In his book, *Conscious Business*, the noted management teacher and consultant, Fred Kofman writes on 'what would a conscious business look like', in this way:

'Quote'

"The most significant observation would be the total absence of abuse, shame, and threat. People would take responsibility for their behaviour and deal with each other honestly and respectfully. They would hold themselves and each other accountable for adhering to some set of agreed-upon values and for working toward an agreed-upon vision. Deviations and errors would be an opportunity for learning and growth, rather than an excuse for blame and punishment.

"There would still be problems, people that don't get along, and losses. A conscious business environment is not a Garden of Eden where everything is always blissful. The marketplace is a turbulent place with no guarantees of success. The main difference displayed by a conscious business environment is that in addition to the drive to achieve their goals, people would experience also the commitment to operate according to their values. This commitment is the source of unconditional dignity that would give the organization and its members a core of luminosity from which to extend into the world.

"A conscious business environment would be a challenge, an invitation to develop people's physical, emotional, mental, and spiritual spheres. The conscious organization is a crucible where people refine themselves through service and partnership. As Kahlil Gibran would say, a conscious business is a place where it becomes obvious that work is 'love made visible'."

How to build such a workplace environment, which fulfills the aspirations of all? It's the role of both the employers and the employees. The employers need to set up sound working conditions and standards; and employees need to follow them. What employers and employees should do to create a pleasant, harmonious workplace as envisaged above, is highlighted in the sections to follow:

Work is Worship

"Work is worship", most religious scriptures say. Every person who earns his livelihood by working honestly is worshipping God. Through our work, we not only support our family and ourselves, we make a big contribution to society. Any job - be it engineer, doctor, secretary, carpenter, truck driver, janitor - when done with integrity and excellence is right livelihood. But if the work is done in an irresponsible or dishonest manner it does not matter what the occupation is, it is not right livelihood. How do you do your work is as important as your occupation. "All labor that uplifts humanity has dignity and importance and should be undertaken with painstaking excellence," said Martin Luther King, Jr.

You must adhere to certain ethics and values at the workplace. In business and in family relationships, remember that the most important things are trust, care and respect for others. Successful workplace relations are built by respecting others, caring and by paying attention to the people around us. Show respect for everyone who works for a living, regardless of how trivial his job. Lack of respect or inattention can damage relationships. "Trust men and they will be true to you; treat them greatly and they will show themselves great," said Ralph Waldo Emerson.

When you arrive at your job in the morning, let the first thing you say brighten everyone's day. Greet people with a smiling face. Begin your work with a sense of prayer. These days, many companies have instituted some sort of prayer to reflect work as worship. Participate in such prayers whole-heartedly. In Reliance Industries, for instance, where I worked for some time, every shift started with a prayer. All meetings, even the board meetings would begin with the prayer. "Believe me, the enterprise that begins with a prayer will end with prosperity, fame and triumph," said Heinrich Von Kleist, the Eighteenth century German poet-novelist.

Be loyal to your boss, your company, and your co-workers. Give the best to your employer. It's one of the best investments you can make. Business is like a game of tennis – those who serve well usually end up winning. Undertake every work in the spirit of ownership - as if this was your personal work, as if you were building your own house. There is a beautiful story that reinforces this concept of ownership at work:

An elderly carpenter was ready to retire. He told his employer-contractor of his plans to leave the house-building business to live a more leisurely life with his wife and enjoy his extended family. He would miss the paycheck each week, but he wanted to retire.

The contractor was sorry to see his good worker go and asked if he could build just one more house as a personal favour. The carpenter said yes, but overtime it was easy to see that his heart was not in his work. He resorted to shoddy workmanship and used inferior materials. It was an unfortunate way to end a dedicated career.

When the carpenter finished his work, his employer came to inspect the house. Then he handed the front-door key to the carpenter and said, "This is your house, my gift to you." The carpenter was shocked! What a shame! If he had only known he was building his own house, he would have done it all so differently.

So it is with us. We do our work, often putting less than our best into it. Then, with a shock, we realise that the boss has given an unsatisfactory annual appraisal. Our attitude and the choices we make today, help build the career we will have tomorrow.

"The deepest principle in human nature is craving to be appreciated," said William James, nineteenth century American doctor and philosopher. People look for appreciation and rewards – salary-increase, promotion, bonus, honour and recognition for the work they do. As employer or manager, you must reward the good work of your people. Never waste an opportunity to compliment good employees and tell them how much they mean to the company. "Everybody likes a compliment," said Abraham Lincoln.

As employees, you do your duty sincerely, and leave the result to God. Sincere work will always be rewarded. Paul Speicher, the noted inspirational writer, puts the theory of work and reward this way: "A law of nature rules that energy cannot be destroyed. You change its form from coal to steam, from steam to power in the turbine, but you do not destroy energy. In the same way, another law governs human activity and rules that honest effort cannot be lost, but that some day the proper benefits will be forthcoming."

Always engage yourself in pleasant behaviours at the workplace. Bad or offensive behaviours can be harmful to you and others around. You can't revert to high school behaviour at the workplace. It can affect how people view you as well as how you perform. In the long run, unpleasant work environment leads to a high turnover and litigation for companies; and stress, psychological or physical health problems for the victims. Here is a list, though not comprehensive, of workplace behaviours, which need to be avoided:

- Littering, spitting, and other unhygienic habits
- Jokes that mock another, including remarks about race, gender

- Taking credit for someone else's work
- Discrimination against inferior occupations
- Using cell phones in mid-conversation or during an appointment
- Behaving aggressively or bullying others
- Blatant misuse of workplace facilities
- Violating workplace safety norms
- Disregard of company's work standards

Love Your Work

Do you remember the quote in the beginning of this chapter? Love your work, it says. Nobody can be successful unless he loves his work. What makes you love your work? A number of things! Foremost, you must have the right skills and attitudes. In this respect, said John D. Rockefeller, II, "The road to happiness lies in two simple principles; find what interests you and that you can do well, and put your whole soul in it – every bit of energy and ambition and natural ability you have." Never say at work that you're tired, angry, or bored. Do your work with full zeal putting your body, mind and soul into it as advised by Rockefeller.

Many people lose zeal in their work when they don't see opportunities for growth in their jobs. During my long industrial career, I have come across many people who lost interest in the work when denied promotion to a higher position. They hated their job, resorted to shoddy work and looked for a change. Some of these people had been my juniors who confided in me their frustration and lack of love for the job. I always advised such people not to be disheartened and lose interest in the work. "Love your work even if the present company is not recognizing your skills. By doing shoddy work you are devaluing your skills and reducing your market value," I used to advise them. Some heeded to my advice, continued working with full steam, and at the same time looked for good opportunities elsewhere.

Don't try to cover up your shortcomings by pretending you know the things; you will only be fooling or deceiving yourself and others. On his first day in the office, a manager not qualified for the new job, was trying to kill time when someone knocked his door. The manager immediately got hold of the telephone, pretending he was busy. He kept talking hi-fi things on the phone to impress the waiting visitor. After completing the call the manager said politely, "Sorry, I kept you waiting for long. It was some important matter. Yes, what can I do for you?" The visitor said, "I just came to connect your telephone, sir."

How long can you pretend and befool others. Such tactics don't last long and sooner or later you would be exposed. You will do well to yourself and the organization by acknowledging your weaknesses and seeking help to improve.

Don't ridicule your work; respect it. While interviewing, the employer said to an applicant, "I'm sorry, things are tight right now, and I have no job for you. I doubt that I could find enough work to keep you busy." The applicant said, "But you have no idea how little work it takes to keep me busy."

Do not get fooled and mislead by the lofty job titles and designations while joining a new organization. These days many companies give employees high profile titles like directors, presidents, vice-presidents and so on, to attract them. After joining the employees find that job responsibilities and or remuneration have no bearing to the title or designation they are holding. They feel they have been cheated by the hollow titles. Over the time, the employees feel they deserve more money than their actual duties merit. But the management thinks it is what you do, not what you are called, that matters. The employees get frustrated, lose love for the job and look for a change.

Maintain Good Communications

Good communication is fundamental to all relationships including that at workplace. Communication does not mean only phones, gadgets, internet, satellites and other facilities linked with sophisticated world-class software, but also a common understanding, tradition, transparency and truthfulness while dealing with the people.

Good and effective communication is the skill of talking with one another, talking from your heart what you feel and mean, saying it clearly and listening with attention what others say. Such a communication should reflect in improved inter-personal relationships at different levels at the workplace, which is an essential ingredient of corporate success. "We have developed communications systems to permit man on the earth to talk with man on the moon. Yet mother often cannot talk with daughter, father to son, black to white, labor with management or democracy with communism," said Hadley Read, American agricultural communication expert.

Whether it is a meeting, instruction, company news, any change in policy, procedures or norms, or whatever, must be based on effective communication. An effective communication is one that is transparent, clearly understood by the people, timely, and two-way flow. As far as possible, written communication should be encouraged. Sometimes, language can be a barrier to effective communication at a workplace where the employees are of multilingual cultures. In such situations, special care needs to be taken to ensure that people understand the medium of communication.

Good communication has to start with listening. Be a good listener. Listening provides a good role model for how you wish to be heard and understood. It's difficult to overestimate the importance of listening or the damage that can result from a failure to listen. Sir Winston Churchill, brave and courageous prime minister of Great Britain who lead his country to victory in the world war, sums up the importance of listening this way: Courage is what it takes to stand up and speak; courage is also what it takes to sit down and listen.

You need to listen through your heart. This becomes evident to the speaker and will help him/her to feel more relaxed, accepted and respected. Be silent and let the other person speak. Allow him to present his views and finish his speech, before you interrupt or intervene. Good listeners need to take in more than just the speakers' words. They need to observe the body language of the speaker, which can give them additional information about the person or the situation. Be present in the dialogue, and don't be distracted by other issues. When the other person has finished, take your turn to be heard. Ask for clarifications, if you have any doubt.

It is said that we Indians are not good listeners. This reminds me of an unpleasant incident. During the final stages of completion of our giant refinery project at Jamnagar during 1998-99, we used to have a meeting of some 15 senior managers every day for about one hour to take stock of the project progress. This meeting used to be chaired by an experienced senior expatriate who had seen through many such projects in his career. Most of the times, these meetings were chaotic. Five-six persons would be talking simultaneously without being heard. Someone was interrupting the other before the later had finished saying what he had to say. The expatriate chairman, not used to this sort of communication was not able to hold people together. One day he was so frustrated that he walked off the meeting angrily remarking, "You Indians don't know how to talk." Some senior managers did not like his remarks and felt insulted. The tussle escalated to the extent that the President of the company had to intervene to calm down the aggrieved.

As said before, good communication is based on truthfulness and openness. People should be encouraged to communicate with each other openly, frankly and truthfully even if it is painful sometimes. Many people are in the habit of saying yes to everyone, knowing very well they can't do what others are asking for. Watch out for people who always say 'yes' to please or satisfy you. The great general Alvaro Obregon of Mexico said, "Don't be afraid of enemies who attack you. Be afraid of the friends who flatter you."

Because of fear or to gain favour, people often agree to whatever the boss says instead of giving the right opinion, and advisors or consultants give false reports. We also need to learn to say 'no', if the situation demands. Being 'Yes-man' all the times does no good. "The art of leadership is saying no, not saying yes. It is very easy to say yes," says Tony Blair, former UK prime minister.

The danger of this 'Yes-manship' in communication is vividly explained in verse 37 of *Sunderkhand* in *Ramcharitmanas*. The verse says, *"Sachiv vaid gur teen Jo priye boliye baeh aas, Raj dharma tan teen kar hoi begai naas."* It means that pleasing words of your minister, teacher or the doctor spoken because of fear, or favour can harm you. The verse refers to the episode when Sri Rama, with his huge army enters Lanka crossing over the ocean. King Ravana who was in the assembly of his wise men asked for their advice how to deal with Rama's advancing army. Fearing his wrath, they all spoke very high of Ravana, praised his valour, and advised him to fight, knowing well he was too weak to face Lord Rama. Overcome by his advisors' flattering words, Ravana fought with the Lord and suffered a fatal defeat.

Nurture Teamwork

Most work is team-based that requires active and sincere participation and cooperation of every member of the team. Teamwork synergises individual skills and competencies and makes an organization excel. Teamwork is the result of cordial relationships at the workplace built by team members through love, compassion and empathy for one another.

However, present-day industrialised society puts a lot of emphasis on individuality, personhood where each person's goals, performance, accountability, rewards, and penalties are the main focus. This philosophy encourages people to think of their own personal interests, how to compete, how to self-protect, how to push others away to become the best, and so on. There is no team spirit and sense of fellow feeling.

While the traditional management philosophy puts primary emphasis on competition, our scriptures give great importance to collaboration and teamwork. Before starting work, people used to pray to God for unity in their endeavours. The following Vedic mantra symbolises the spirit of teamwork:

> Om, saha naavavtu
>
> Saha nau bhunaktu
>
> Saha veeryam Karavaa-vahai
>
> Teja-svi naa-vadheeta-mastu
>
> Maa vidvishaa-vahai

In simple translation the mantra means: May God protect us both, May He nourish us both, May we both work together with great energy, May our study be thorough and fruitful, May we never hate each other.

Lack of trust and appreciation, and poor communications are some important factors for low teamwork in an organization. Some HR experts also blame the annual ritual of 'performance review' for the damaging effects it has on the team work. Performance reviews are supposed to provide an objective evaluation that helps determine pay and rewards, and lets employees know

where they can do better. But the manner they are conducted, the experts say, fosters a destructive relationship between the boss and the subordinate that lowers morale, kills teamwork and hurts the productivity. The boss in the performance review thinks himself or herself as the evaluator, and doesn't engage in teamwork with the subordinate. It isn't, "How are we going to work together as a team?" "How are you performing for me?" It's not our joint performance that's at issue. It's the employee's performance that's a problem.

At a workplace where teamwork is low, people often try to play foul to get credit for work done by others. "My grandfather once told me that there were two kinds of people: those who do the work and those who take the credit. He told me to try to do be in the first group; there was much less competition," said Indira Gandhi.

"There is no limit to what can be accomplished if it does not matter who gets the credit," said Ralph Waldo Emerson, nineteenth century American philosopher. There is a joke how a boss tries to get the credit to himself of his subordinate's idea:

A boss said to his employee: "Thank you for giving me this idea, which I have borrowed and made better." "How did you do that?" responded the employee. "By attaching my name to it," replied the boss.

Sometimes we kill the spirit of teamwork by our authoritative and egoistic approach at the workplace. A boss after overriding the decision of a task force that he created to find a solution to a problem: "I'm sorry if I ever gave you the impression your input would have any effect on my decision for the outcome of this project!"

Establish Realistic Work Standards

Realistic workplace standards help both the employees and the organization. These standards or norms may be in the area of productivity, quality, health and safety, environment protection, human relations, customer service and so on. Employers should ensure that the standards are made, updated periodically and communicated to the employees. And on the part of employees, they should welcome such work standards and follow them faithfully, instead of rejecting them because they harm their interests.

Quite often, employees oppose new technology, automation, and modernisation unless management takes appropriate efforts to motivate them before hand. Before introducing changes that may directly or indirectly affect people, it is important that they should be appraised and consulted appropriately, trained and motivated to accept the changes. The people should be taken into confidence and convinced that the changes are in their benefit. "All of us perform better and more willingly when we know why we're doing what we have been told or asked to do," says Zig Ziglar, the noted American author and motivational speaker.

Let me share a story of how the employees reacted on an automation scheme in a mining company: Two labourers were watching a new computerized steam shovel at work in an open-pit mine. The shovel took in a truckload of dirt in one big bite. After just a few bites, the truck was full. One labourer said to the other, "Man that machine has put five hundred of us out of work. It's our enemy." The other man said, "Yes, and if got rid of our shovels, we could create a million jobs for people to dig the mine with spoons." Did you notice how motivated employees react so differently than the unmotivated?

But if the company has ruthless policies, impossible standards or targets to be met, it is impossible to convince people to follow them. Take for instance, a new efficiency push some retailers in US are experimenting with to improve productivity. As per a Wall Street Journal's report, retailers are using computer programmes to schedule workers more efficiently. The programme finds out how long it should take for employees to complete a sale - three seconds to greet a customer, two minutes to help someone trying on clothing, 30 seconds to fold a sweater, and so on. The goal of the programme is to find out the number of employees needed in a store at any given time, based on customer traffic.

Now, many employees are unhappy about the new efficiency push. They feel the system leaves them with shorter shifts, makes it difficult to schedule their lives, and unleashes Darwinian forces on the sales floor that damage morale. In the current financial meltdown, we may see many companies taking similar initiatives that harm employees' interests.

Balancing Work and Family

Stephan Covey, the famous management guru, stresses the importance of family and work in his book, *Seven Habits of Highly Effective People*. He rightly says no success can compensate for failure in the home. Managers must learn to strike a balance between work and family.

Indira Nooyi, Indian born, CEO of beverage giant Pepsi Co., named fifth most powerful women in the world by Forbes Magazine, finds it difficult at times to balance her family life with her high profile career. During a discussion on 'Women and Global Leadership', organized by confederation of Indian Industry and the Yale Club in 2008 in New York, Nooyi, said, "I am a mother first, then a CEO, then a wife. The other day my 14-year old daughter sent me an e-mail asking for an hour's appointment with me. The confusion and the worries over whether I am doing justice, make me tear my head. You want to be a mother, at the same time you have to take care of your career also."

No doubt, a balanced work and family life depends, to a large extent, on employees' personal values, priorities and choices in life; there are a number of ways a company can help its employees to achieve that balance. Indeed, a balanced work and home life not only helps employees lead a happy life, but also gives immense dividends to employers. It is in the employers' own enlightened self-interest to provide wherever practical, facilities like housing, schooling, medical, child-care, cooperative stores, flexi-timing, vacations, maternity leave and so on that save employees a lot of hardship and inconvenience. Happy and loyal employees will always go the extra mile.

Providing the above-mentioned facilities to employees is not a new idea. Many companies in the past had been doing this as an integral part of employment. But as the companies started focusing only on their core businesses, such practices lost their significance. However, the same are getting revived again through CSR and other corporate initiatives.

Bhaskar Das, executive director, Times Group speaking at the presentation of "Best Workplaces 2008' awards in Mumbai said, "India has moved from an economy that had a cost advantage to one that has become the talent hunting ground for fortune 500 companies. Therefore, in our times, it is not a luxury to have robust people management practices, it is the key."

After Bhopal Gas disaster in 1985, I visited major industrial units in Madhya Pradesh for a safety audit. This gave me an opportunity to see many workplaces closely. I was surprised to see the extent of employees' facilities in a major industrial unit, manufacturing synthetic fibre, in the state. It had a beautiful housing complex with sprawling lawns and playgrounds, a well-managed high school, two temples, a big hospital and several other community services. I was especially attracted by the company's hospital in the township. It was a wonderful, well equipped, thirty-five specialties hospital. I asked the CEO of the company whether they were running a viscose fibre plant or a hospital. "Both," the CEO said jokingly, "health and well-being of employees is our major concern and being at a remote place, it will be hard for them to get timely medical attention. When people are at work, we don't want them to be unnecessarily worried about someone who may be sick at home. They can leave their worries to the medical department and concentrate on their work." He added that their hospital also catered to the needs of general community in the neighbourhood as also from distant places. Later, I learnt that was a very popular charity hospital in the area run by the company for the benefit of its employees and the general public.

When Ambani's were planning to put up a major grass-roots refinery at Jamnagar, Gujarat, in 1995, they had initially no plans of setting up any employees' housing and other social facilities. It was hard for the experts to convince the owners that such facilities were necessary to attract good people to work in the refinery, located in a remote area, 30 km from the city. However, good sense prevailed upon the owners and they decided to put up housing and other infrastructure even before major work on the refinery construction started. And it paid well. Today, a 500 acres world-class township, called 'Reliance Greens' sits adjoining the refinery site. With its beautiful houses, lush green gardens, a top-class school, a well-equipped hospital, sports stadium, Olympic-size swimming pool, five-star guesthouses, club, gym, temple and other facilities, 'Reliance Greens' dwarfs any modern city.

Employees are very happy to have all the facilities for a comfortable life next door to their workplace. Even those who were sceptical of the idea of having the township now believe it was a good decision. In one of the company's AGM held in the township, shareholders were greatly impressed by the management's foresight to build the township. One investor was heard saying jokingly, "If the oil business goes down tomorrow, we will still have a beautiful real estate business."

Child-care is a big problem especially with couples both of whom are working and have no one else at home to look after the small children. The high cost of quality child-care and all the shuttling around to leave small children in day-care centres may be very taxing for the couple. Such employees often find it hard to achieve a balanced work and home life. Companies can do a great service to their employees by providing on-site child-care facilities at affordable cost.

Flexible work schedule is another facility that helps employees in many ways, especially in big cities. Some companies are already following it. "Workers are struggling to handle child and elder care needs, further their education, and play a role in their communities, all of which are responsibilities that operate on unpredictable hours. At the same time, many CEOs are looking for more productivity and commitment and less absenteeism from a workforce. Flexible work arrangements hit on all of those needs," says Susan Seitel, President of Work & Family Connection Inc. USA.

Handling Workplace Stress

At the present times, stress has become an epidemic at the workplace inflicting people from shop floor to the boardroom. It affects people in many ways, including their health, relationships and performance at the workplace. While most of us have learnt to live with work-related stress, few are aware that stress is a silent killer. People even in their 20s are falling prey to conditions like obesity, diabetes, heart problems, back injuries, arthritis and others. Chronic fatigue, irritability, short temper, aching muscles, sleeplessness, and loss of appetite are some symptoms of stress. As per National Institute for Occupational Safety and Health, some job conditions that lead to stress include:

- Heavy workload, infrequent rest breaks, long work hours and shift work
- Hectic and routine tasks that don't utilise the employee's skills
- Little sense of control over the job performed
- Lack of participation in decision making
- Poor communications in the organization
- Poor family-friendly policies
- Poor interpersonal relations and lack of support from colleagues
- Job insecurity
- Lack of opportunity for growth, advancement, or promotion
- Poor environmental conditions - noise, air pollution, ergonomic problems

Improving the above conditions will eliminate the basic factors that cause stress at the workplace. However, the fast-paced life of 21st century, globalization, work pressures, tight deadlines and cut throat competition may not allow many companies to create ideal working conditions. The '24x7-isation of workplace' is burning out workforce. Therefore, it is pertinent that we learn to cope up with stress. How do we do that?

There are many destressing techniques available, which include exercise, yoga, and meditation. Yoga and meditation are booming on-site stress busters. Many companies, worldwide are becoming increasingly proactive to use yoga and meditation as very effective tools to manage workplace stress. These holistic techniques help build a good working environment, foster teamwork, motivate and make employees more focused and proactive, and increase productivity. Indian companies like NHPC, NTPC, SAIL, Thermax, Kirloskar Engines, and many 500 fortune international companies including General Motors, Deutshe bank, Coca-cola Co, IBM etc. are using yoga and meditation to destress their workforce.

Yoga is not only changing the workplace ambience, but is also changing sensitive employees into much tolerant people. It brings in them a total transformation of behaviour and outlook to work, family and society. Some people pride themselves on never changing, even when the world around them is changing. Their mind is like concrete, mixed up and permanently set. Yoga makes them flexible, bodily as well as mentally.

"If we can help people feel better and think better, no matter where they are in the company chain, they will feel better and start contributing a lot better; then the entire company will start to work better," says Tevis Gale, owner of yoga consultancy firm 'Balance Integration Corporation' in New York City.

Sunder Shridhar, manager, programme management office, Unisys Global Services India says, "Yoga works effectively as an employee retention tool as it motivates employees to come to work and feel good about it."

My own experience of conducting yoga-based human resource development programmes in many companies has been very encouraging. My one-day workshop on "Stress management by yoga" for corporate executives has been received very well in many companies during the last few years. Here is what some participants said after attending the workshop:

"It was found very informative and participants took good interest in knowing the different dimension of stress and ways to manage it. The practical session of yoga *'asana'* and *'pranayam'* was well received by our employees and they are even practising now"...Amar Jha, General Manager, Niko Resources, Surat.

"The workshop helped us to realise the potentials of yoga in providing a stress-free, healthy and happy life. We will all live a better life because of your help. The handouts and your book on *The Joy of Living by Yoga* received by all the participants would serve as a useful resource to continue practicing what was taught in the workshop."...Christ Iatropulos, CEO, Kieh Co., Chicago, USA.

"Thanks for spreading the noble message of yoga among our employees. The yoga workshops held in the refinery will help employees to recognize, prevent, and cure various health hazards specific to their occupations." ...BM Bansal, Executive Director, IOC, Mathura Refinery.

9

Relationship with God

> Spiritual Relationship is far more precious than physical.
> Physical relationship divorced from spiritual is body without soul
>
> *Mahatma Gandhi*

So far we discussed building worldly relationships. In this chapter we will talk about relationship with God, a relationship that is very special and divine. This relationship is unique and different for everyone. It is the most intimate and personal connection you will ever experience. No other man, woman, child or friend can come between you and God.

Relationship with God! My God, my Lord, my father, my mother, my swami, and my saviour - words like these have no meaning for people who don't believe in God, spirituality or some higher power. Such people can't relate themselves with God in any way. For them, the mere idea of relationship with God is a farce.

While I was talking to a new friend on the subject of relationship with God: "Nonsense! He said indignantly, "How can you relate to someone who does not even exist?" "What do you mean God does not exist!" I responded in awe. "Show me where is God," he asked. "He is everywhere, He is omnipresent, omnipotent and omniscient. " I replied. "But I don't see him. If there was any God, there won't be so much chaos and suffering in the world," he reacted sharply. I got his point. Like Abraham Lincoln who once said, "I can see how it might be possible for a man to look down upon the earth and be an atheist, but I cannot see how he could look up into the heavens and say there is no God," I tried to convince my friend that God does exist in spite of all the mess around us.

Now, my challenge was to show God to my friend before I talk of any relationship with Him. But how were I to show God to my friend when I myself have not seen Him! Well, my concept of God is different. For me, and for that reason for most of those who don't doubt His existence, God is a force, and a force cannot be seen, it is felt. Christopher Morley, the noted American poet said: Men talk of "finding God," but no wonder it is difficult; He is hidden in the darkest hiding-place, your heart. You yourself are a part of Him.

God Does Exist

"Isavasyam idam sarvam," God is present here everywhere, our scripture tell us. Yes, God exists but can't be seen directly. We see Him through His wonderful creation - the numerous species of life, the rivers, the mountains, the stars, and many other seen and unseen things of the cosmos. Take for instance, the human body itself. There are around seventy five trillion cells in our body. If these cells are stacked one above the other, can you imagine how high the stack will go? No, probably it is beyond your comprehension. It will be hard for you to believe that the stack will reach the moon! Human brain, the most powerful

computer ever made. Our heart, a highly sophisticated pump that never tires, pumps 15000 litres of blood - enough to fill 40,000 cans of coke every day. There are around 160,000 kilometers of arteries and veins, circulating blood in our body - enough to circle the earth four times. These are just few wonders of the human body. There are many more and highly complex systems in His vast creation, which reflect Gods existence.

> Why we have so many temples, if god is everywhere? A wise man said: Air is everywhere, but we still need a fan to feel it.

The myriad creation, which appears so solid and real, is only an idea in the mind of God, frozen into physical forms. The question is not 'Where is God'? But, where He is not?' Albert Einstein said, "When I read Bhagwad Gita and reflected about how God created this universe everything else seems superfluous."

Yoga guru, Baba Ramdev says, "My existence is being regulated by an invisible power and I consider that power as God. I think those who deny the existence of God are illogical, unscientific and unenlightened. I believe God is not merely a deity or idol. I view the power which is controlling all the activities of the universe as God."

Superstar and Badshah of Indian cinema, Shah Rukh Khan says, "I am always praying in my heart. I don't seek God. I find Him in everything and everywhere."

Though God is omnipresent and all pervading, our ignorance does not allow us to see Him. Ravindra Kumar Karnani translated an old Hindi poem on our inability to see God:

> The child whispered, 'God, speak to me'
> And a meadowlark sang.
> The child did not hear.

So the child yelled, 'God, speak to me!'
And the thunder rolled across the sky,
but the child did not listen.
The child looked around and said,
'God let me see you' and a star shone brightly,
but the child did not notice.

And the child shouted,
'God show me a miracle!'
And a life was born but the child did not know.

So the child cried out in despair,
'Touch me God, and let me know you are here!'
Whereupon God reached down, and touched the child.
But the child brushed the butterfly away,
and walked away unknowingly.

God does exist, but the trouble is we don't seek Him. Allow me to narrate a story from an e-mail forward to prove the point. A man went to a barbershop to have his hair cut and his beard trimmed. As the barber began to work, they began to have a good conversation. They talked about so many things and various subjects. When they eventually touched on the subject of God, the barber said: "I don't believe that God exists."

"Why do you say that?" asked the customer.

"Well, you just have to go out in the street to realise that God doesn't exist. Tell me, if God exists, would there be so many sick people? Would there be abandoned children? If God existed, there would be neither suffering nor pain. I can't imagine a loving God who would allow all of these things," replied the barber.

The customer thought for a moment, but didn't respond because he didn't want to start an argument. The barber finished his job and the customer left the shop. Just after he left the barbershop, he saw a man in the street with long, stringy, dirty hair and an untrimmed beard. He looked dirty and unkempt. The customer turned back and entered the barber shop again and he said to the barber: "You know what? Barbers do not exist."

"How can you say that?" asked the surprised barber. "I am here, and I am a barber. And I just worked on you!"

"No!" the customer exclaimed. "Barbers don't exist because if they did, there would be no people with dirty long hair and untrimmed beards, like that man outside."

"Ah, but barbers do exist! That's what happens when people do not come to me!"

"Exactly!" affirmed the customer. "That's the point! God, too, does exist! That's what happens when people do not go to Him and seek His help. That's why there's so much pain and suffering in the world."

Your Relationship with God

How would you relate to God? Your relationship with God is a personal matter and depends on how you perceive Him. There is a beautiful verse in Tulsidas' *Ramcharitmanas*: *"Ja ki rei bhavna jesi, prabhu murat dekhi tin tesi,"* which means you see God the way you feel. This verse refers to the Sita swyamvara, where king Janaka had invited a host of kings and princes to win his daughter, Sita in marriage. The condition was that Sita would garland the prince who would break the mighty divine bow of lord Shiva placed on the dais in the centre of the grand marriage pavilion.

A large gathering of princes from distant places, members of the royal family, distinguished guests and subjects had assembled in the pavilion for the grand spectacle. As Sri Rama, who was also invited as one of the eligible contestants for marriage, entered the pavilion, everybody's attention got focused on this God-incarnate, handsome prince of Ayodhya.

Different people saw Lord Rama differently. King Janaka and his queen Sunaina perceived him as their potential son-in-law, but feared if he could break the bow. Sita perceived him as her darling husband and wished him success in the competition. The young women in the gathering wished Rama to be their brother-in-law who would visit them often if he weds Sita, but doubted whether his tender hands would break the mighty bow. Among the contestants present, some mighty, proud princes looked at Rama with vanity, perceived him as their potential enemy and vowed to defeat him in the competition. And some humble and good-hearted among them adored Rama as their friend, leader and wished him success.

In this way, different people in the grand assembly related themselves to Rama, the embodiment of God according to their feelings. Likewise, each one of us has his particular relationship with God, though, sadly, in this materialistic world, most have forgotten that eternal tie.

Now, how you perceive God, and relate yourself to Him. We can be in relationship with God as a friend, parent, child, lover, servant, master, teacher, and so on. Any relationship with God is essentially based on *Bhakti*, the profound and eternal love for Him. *Bhakti* is love of God, but also the expression and blossoming of love in all our relationships. The divine light of God resides in all that is alive, or for that matter, even that which is lifeless. Through our relationships with others we discover our love for God. Those in relationship with God are called *Bhaktas* or devotees.

Arjuna, the great hero of the Mahabartha was a devotee in relationship with God as a friend. His friendship was different from friendship in the mundane world. His friendship was transcendental and divine. Arjuna who was a great devotee of his friend, Krishna accepted him as pure, supreme, Godhead.

Mirabai, queen of Mewar was a devotee of God as a passionate lover. She considered Lord Krishna her divine husband right from her childhood. Even after being married to Rana of Mewar, she continued her spiritual partnership with God in spite of great resistance from the members of the royal family. She was subjected to a lot of hardships to forsake Krishna as her husband, but her love for Lord Krishna was immortal. She composed and sang numerous loving songs in praise of the Lord, which are very popular even today. She put her unconditional love for Krishna in these words:

> Unbreakable, O Lord,
>
> Is the love
>
> That binds me to you:
>
> Like diamond, it breaks the hammer that strikes it.

King Dashratha saw Lord as his son. In an earlier birth as Mannu with wife, Shatrupai, he performed immense penance in praise of Lord Vishnu. The Lord appeared before them and blessed the couple with a boon. They asked, "Lord, if you are really pleased, bless us with a son like your own self." So, Lord Vishnu fulfilled their desire by incarnating as Rama, the divine child of king Dashratha and queen Kaushalya in a later birth. Dashratha's love for his son Lord Rama was so profound and intense that he gave up his life after Rama went to forests as ordained by his stepmother Kaikayi.

Hanuman was a devotee of God as a servant or *sevak*. He is known and praised for his selfless service to his master, Lord Rama. When Hanuman returned to Sri Rama after finding Sitaji in Lanka, the Lord was so pleased with him that He said, "Hanuman, you have done so much for me that I am indebted to you for ever."

Jesus Christ is known as the most beloved Son of God who came in this world to save people from their sins and sufferings. The cross of Jesus is the supreme evidence of the love of God.

Mahatma Gandhi put the relationship with God this way:

> To me, God is Truth and Love;
>
> God is ethics and morality;
>
> God is fearlessness.
>
> God is the source of Light and Life and yet He is above and beyond all these.
>
> God is conscience...
>
> He is a personal God to those who need His personal presence.
>
> He is embodied to those who need His touch.
>
> He is the purest essence.
>
> He simply is to those who have faith.
>
> He is all things to all men.

Deepen Your Faith

Like any other relationship, relationship with God is based on deep faith, unfailing trust and unconditional love. Leo Tolstoy puts relationship with God this way:

> Where there is faith, there is love;
>
> Where there is love, there is peace;
>
> Where there is peace, there is God;
>
> And where there is God, there is no need.

Webster partially defines faith as an unquestioning belief in God with complete trust, confidence and reliance. "Faith is an oasis in the heart which can never be reached by the caravan of thinking," said Kahlil Gibran. Faith or spirituality can be described as a personal quest for meaning and purpose in life. It usually leads to the discovery of a higher power - call it God, *Ishwara*, Allah, Spirit or whatever, which helps the individual to experience hope, love, peace, and understanding. This discovery also contributes to the formation of our inner belief system. Our faith in God is reinforced when we see and appreciate His myriad creation.

Faith is very subjective. One can have faith in an idol, a stone, a saint, a living God, or an unknown higher power. Life without faith would be very difficult. Faith makes the material world easier to deal with. "There is nothing that wastes the body like worry, and one who has any faith in God should be ashamed to worry about anything," said Mahatma Gandhi. Faith gives you the mental strength, stability and wisdom to face the lure of temptation for money, fame and success, which are all temporary.

Faith makes us better humans. Having faith in God is like always having a fatherly or motherly presence with us. When you have that presence with you, like a little child walking with his parents, you won't be scared by even the biggest and nastiest dogs. "But for my faith in God, I should have been a raving maniac," said Mahatma Gandhi.

Faith should not be confused with religion, which is an organisational aspect of faith. Religion can be described as the external of our faith system. This is more of a social, a corporate endeavour in which people, by belonging to a group or organization that adheres to certain beliefs and practices, find meaning and purpose.

It is very important for each one of us to acknowledge the presence of the Divine Power in every good or bad situation. But we are so engrossed in our own lives that we forget that whatever is happening is because of some supernatural power.

Although, most of us, at some point of time feel the presence of God but still keep questioning His existence. Whenever things go bad, we come to a conclusion that there is no God. Just because things did not go our way, we cannot blame God. Perhaps, we did not act the way God wanted or we lacked faith in Him. "All who call on God in true faith, earnestly from the heart, will certainly be heard, and will receive what they have asked and desired," said Martin Luther.

An unfailing faith in God does not mean that we sit idle and look towards Him for help. We need to put our best efforts. As Captain S S Kohli, the pilot who miraculously saved 170 passengers of Flight IC 866 at Mumbai Airport on 14 February 2009, said, "I believe there is an omnipresent God who answers our good deeds. Every day, we should devote some time to prayers. That helps me, not just during the near-miss incident at Mumbai airport, but also in other aspects of my life. Every thing in my life has been smooth because of Him. But God is there not just to give, you also have to work hard."

Our life is like the game of cards. The deal you get in the shuffle is your destiny, the hand of God, but the way you play the deal is your freewill, your efforts. In spite of a good deal, you may lose the game if you don't play your hand properly. On the contrary you may win even a poorly dealt hand if you play intelligently. So is with our faith in God. We may have great faith, but that will not help if we sit idle.

According to a newspaper report, the University of Oxford researchers will spend nearly $4 million to study why mankind embraces God. The grant to the Ian Ramsey Center for Science and Religion will bring anthropologists, theologians, philosophers and other academics together for three years to study whether belief in a divine being is a basic part of mankind's makeup. "There are a lot of issues. What is it that is innate in human nature to believe in God, whether it is gods or something superhuman or supernatural?" said Roger Trigg, acting director of the centre. The study will be funded by the John Templeton Foundation, a US-based philanthropic organization, that funds wide-ranging research into questions that deal with the laws of nature and issues of spirituality. He said, research suggests that faith in God is a universal human impulse found in most cultures around the world, even though it has been waning in Britain and Western Europe.

Trust in God

We shall overcome all difficulties and steer safely through every storm, provided our trust is fixed on God. "All I have seen teaches me to trust the Creator for all I have not seen," said Ralph Waldo Emerson, the great American philosopher. Let me share with you a beautiful story from Mahabharata, the classic Hindu epic, telling how God takes care of our needs when we have unfailing trust in him:

A poor man and his wife lived in a remote village. As a petty daily-wager, he hardly made both ends meet. He was a simple and pious devotee of Lord Krishna, and read Bhagavad Gita every day. One morning, while he was studying the Gita, his wife pleaded that he must find work today, and bring some food, as there was not a grain left in the house. The poor man was absorbed in reading the verse 9.22 of *Bhagavad Gita* in which, Lord Krishna says that He looks after the needs of those who worship Him with devotion. As the poor man read those lines, doubt about the truth of the Lord's promise arose in his mind momentarily. He drew a red line under the words to remind him to think about the matter later, and left in search of work.

After a while when the poor man was away, the wife heard a knock at the door. As she opened the door, she saw a handsome young lad standing at the door asking for help to take off the heavy basket he was carrying on his head. As the wife helped the boy to put the basket off his head, she was astonished to see the basket full of grains, fruits and vegetables, "Your husband has sent all this," the boy said. As the boy bent to lower the basket, she saw blood oozing out of wounds on his back. "How did you get injured my boy," she said. "Your husband hit me with a stick when I hesitated to carry the heavy basket, and asked me to hurry up and deliver the basket to you," the boy said, murmuring." She felt pity on the boy and asked him to wait as she went inside to bring a piece of cloth to clean and dress up his wound. When she came out, she found the boy had already disappeared. She was perplexed and waited anxiously for her husband to return and tell all what happened.

Weird and frustrated, the poor man returned home in the evening, and told his wife he could not buy any food, as he did not get any work. "But you sent so much food through that young boy in the morning! And why did you beat him," said the wife. For a moment, the poor man was perplexed, but soon understood the entire mystery. "That boy was none other than Lord Himself who came in the guise of a handsome lad to fulfill His promise to His sincere devotees," exclaimed the poor man.

Loving God

"To fall in love with God is the greatest of all romances; To seek him, the greatest adventure; To find him, the greatest achievement," said composer - musician Raphael Simon. God's ability to love us is limited only by our ability to receive that love. God loves us unconditionally, but many times we don't understand His love. Mary Stevenson describes God's unconditional love in her beautiful poem, 'Footprints in the Sand':

> One night I had a dream.
>
> I dreamed I was walking along the beach with the Lord...
>
> Across the sky flashed scenes from my life...

For each scene, I noticed two sets of footprints in the sand,
one belonging to me, and the other to the Lord...
When the last scene of my life flashed before me,

I looked back at the footprints in the sand.
I noticed that many times along the path of my life there was only one set of footprints.
I also noticed that it happened at the very lowest
and saddest times in my life.
This really bothered me and I questioned the Lord about it: "Lord, you said that once I decided to follow you,
you'd walk with me all the way. But I have noticed that during the most troublesome times in my life there is only one set of footprints.
I don't understand why
when I need you most you would leave me."
The Lord replied:
"My precious child, I love you and would never leave you.
During your times of trial and suffering,
when you see only one set of footprints, it was then
that I carried you."

It is true that God's love is all pervading and no one can live or survive without such love. However, due to our ignorance we are wandering around like a child lost in a wonderland without its mother.

Sri Chinmoy Swami said:

> You may not know,
> But it is true:
> With each heartbeat
> Your heart is calling; 'God, God!'
> You may not hear it,
> But God Himself definitely hears
> Your heart's cry.

God is the source from where we all come, because of Him we exist, and someday we all return to Him. The core desire of everyone in this world is to have eternal happiness, peace and love even though he may be looking for it in wrong things, places or people. Man has not, and cannot find that eternal joy and love with all his knowledge, wealth, technology, science, and art, etc. As long as we are running after these worldly things, God's love keeps eluding us, and we feel miserable.

Remember our time on earth is limited, and we are not going to live here forever. When we contemplate that we will leave this world sooner or later empty handed, money, material possessions, name and fame lose their meaning. We can't take them with us and certainly they have no place in the next 'world'.

So, what are you waiting for? Become a perfect lover of God forming a relationship of your own with Him - husband, wife, friend, father, mother, master, child or whatever. Experience the true love of God, which cannot be described but can be felt without a doubt. Without the experience of God's love, we remain like a barren land, fruit tree without fruits, a river without water and a mother without a child. Such a life cannot provide the eternal happiness or joy and peace we all are striving for.

God can be conceived in whatever name and form we choose. He can be even formless. For most worldly people, it may be difficult to follow the steep path of saints, scholars or yogis to conceive God. But we can certainly follow the path of *bhakti* or love; the path followed by *gopis*, the shepherd girls of *vrindaban*. One such perfect *gopi* was Radha who was reborn as Mira, both being the perfect examples of divine love.

Another way to love God is to love His creation. Respect every living being as God. "To love another person is to see the face of God," said Victor Hugo, the nineteenth century French poet-statesman. In his innocent prayer, a child said to God, "I bet it is hard for you to love everybody in the whole world. There are only four people in our family and I can never do it." "If you don't find God in the next person you meet, it is waste of time looking for Him further," said Mahatma Gandhi.

Be Humble, Don't Challenge God

On his views about God and spirituality, the former Indian president, APJ Kalam said, "When I look up into the sky, I see a million stars. One star - the sun - is enough to keep our whole solar system running. We are yet to discover how many more solar systems are there. The thought is overwhelming! It makes me realise that we are just specks in the universe. It gives me reason to believe that there is something, somewhere that I can turn to. And so, I pray."

Pankaj Advani, 23, the holder of five world titles in billiards says, "I am a firm believer in God. My faith and my respect for God keeps me grounded, no matter what I achieve in life."

AR Rahman, the noted Indian composer who got two Oscars in 2009 for Slumdog Millionaire, said, "I am like a boat without an oar. I let life take its own course. I know only my work and God. I pray a lot. You get dejected if you plan something and it does not happen. But if you just let life take its course..."

There are many other great people like these who consider God as supreme commander and attribute their achievements to Him without any feeling of pride or arrogance. Did you notice the humility of president Kalam in his admission of man's limitations? Yes, we are indeed, too small and weak in comparison to the infinite power of God who is omnipotent, omnipresent and omniscient. Unfortunately, many people are so arrogant and proud of themselves and their achievements that they challenge even God's existence or His actions. They forget what St Francis of Assisi once said, "You can only do what the hand of God allows you to do."

Here are some real-life stories that speak of the incredible power of God and helplessness of humankind in comparison:

Tancredo Neves (President of Brazil)

During the Presidential campaign, he said if he got 500,000 votes from his party, not even God would remove him from Presidency.

Sure he got the votes, but he got sick a day before being made President, then he died.

Cazuza (Brazilian composer, singer and poet):

During a show in Canecio (Rio de Janeiro), while smoking his cigarette, he puffed out some smoke into the air and said: 'God, that's for you.'

He died at the age of 32 of lung cancer in a horrible manner.

The man who built the Titanic

After the construction of Titanic, a reporter asked him how safe the Titanic would be.

With an ironic tone he said: 'Not even God can sink it'

The result: I think you all know what happened to the Titanic. It sank killing more than 1500 people.

Marilyn Monroe (Actress)

She was visited by Billy Graham during a presentation of a show.

He said the Spirit of God had sent him to preach to her.

After hearing what the Preacher had to say, she said: 'I don't need your Jesus'.

A week later, she was found dead in her apartment

Campinas (Brazil)

In 2005 in Campinas, Brazil a group of drunken friends went to pick up a girl friend from her house.

The mother accompanied her to the car and was so worried about the drunkenness of her friends and she said to the daughter holding her hand, who was already seated in the car: "My daughter, go with God, and He May protect you."

She responded: "Only if He (God) travels in the trunk, 'cause inside here it's already full"

Hours later, news came by that they had been involved in a fatal accident, everyone had died. The car could not be recognized what type of car it had been, but surprisingly, the trunk was intact. The police said there was no way the trunk could have remained intact. To their surprise, inside the trunk was a crate of eggs none was broken.

So let's be humble and not challenge God. "Humble yourselves therefore under the mighty hand of God. That may exalt you in due time: Casting all your care upon him; for he careth for you," says the Bible. And always remember the advice of St. Patrick: "May the strength of God pilot us, may the wisdom of God instruct us, may the hand of God protect us, may the word of God direct us."

We should firmly believe that whatever happens, it happens with the will of God, and man has no control over it. Let me share a beautiful verse (51.4, Balkand) of *Ramcharitmanas* that affirms this belief. It says: *"Hoee hai voee jo Ram ruchi raakha, ko kari tark bdavey saakha," meaning* whatever Lord Rama wishes will happen, therefore what is the use in arguing or debating over the happening.

Thank God for His Blessings

We should be grateful to God for what we have in our life. Every day should be a day of thanksgiving for the gifts of life: Sunshine, water, food, and all the things we need. When we say thank you God, we open our eyes to all the miracles around us and establish a relationship with Him, their creator. Wake up being thankful for each new day. Thanksgiving and praise open in our consciousness, the way for spiritual growth.

Gratitude is one of the great positive emotions. It creates magnetism. A magnet draws things to itself, and, therefore, giving heartfelt thanks for all the good around us makes us attract more good into our daily lives. Counting our blessings and giving thanks to God every day invokes generosity in us, forming an antidote to many negative emotions that colour our perception. Bollywood icon, Shah Rukh Khan expresses his gratitude to God in this way: "Allah has given me so much love through my fans and the people around me, I couldn't have asked for bigger blessings! I have no fear, because I believe in God."

"The breeze of grace is always blowing on you. You have to open the sails and your boat will move forward," said

Ramakrishna Paramhansa. God's bounties are endless, but the trouble with us is we don't acknowledge His blessings. Let me share with you one of the good e-mails I received from a friend, which is so true in our own lives:

I dreamt that I went to Heaven and an angel was showing me around. We walked side-by-side inside a large workroom filled with angels. My angel guide stopped in front of the first section and said, "This is the 'Receiving Section'. Here, all petitions to God said in prayer are received."

I looked around in this area, and it was terribly busy with so many angels sorting out petitions written on voluminous paper sheets and scraps from people all over the world.

Then we moved down on a long corridor until we reached the second section. The angel then said to me, "This is the 'Packaging and Delivery Section'. Here, the graces and blessings the people asked for are processed and delivered to the living persons who asked for them."

I noticed again how busy it was there. There were many angels working hard at that station, since so many blessings had been requested and were being packaged for delivery to Earth.

Finally at the farthest end of the long corridor we stopped at the door of a very small station. To my great surprise, only one angel was seated there, idly doing nothing. "This is the 'Acknowledgment Section,' my angel friend quietly admitted to me. He seemed embarrassed. "How is it that there is no work going on here?" I asked.

"So sad," the angel sighed. "After people receive the blessings that they asked for, very few send back acknowledgments."

"How does one acknowledge God's blessings?" I asked.

"Simple," the angel answered. Just say, "Thank you, Lord."

"What blessings should they acknowledge?" I asked.

The angel gave me a long list of blessings to be acknowledged. However, on waking up, I forgot many of them. That is what happens with most of us when we forget to thank God for all the wonderful things that are present in our life. Let's not forget to be grateful to God and thank Him for all His blessings. Sometimes things may not be the best as you wished. Don't despair. Be grateful to Him, you may be still better than many others. For instance:

Be thankful if you have food, clothes on your back, a roof overhead and a place to sleep; you are richer than 75% of this world.

Be thankful if you woke up this morning with more health than illness; you are more blessed than the many who will not even survive this day.

Should you notice a streak of grey hair in the mirror; be thankful and think of the cancer patient in chemo who wishes she had hair to examine.

I cried that I had no shoes until I met a person who had no feet. Thank God I have the feet.

Should you despair over a relationship turned bad, think of the person who has never known what it's like to love and be loved in return. Thank God, you are still in relationship.

If you find yourself stuck in traffic, don't despair. Be thankful, there are people in this world for whom driving is an unheard privilege.

If you have never experienced the fear in battle, the loneliness of imprisonment, the agony of torture, or the pangs of starvation; thank God, you are ahead of 700 million people in the world.

If you can hold your head up and smile, you are not the norm, you're unique to all those in doubt and despair.

If you have a bad day at work, think of the man who has been out of work for years. And if you grieve the passing of another weekend, think of the woman in dire straits, working twelve hours a day, seven days a week to feed her children.

Should you find yourself at a loss and pondering what is life all about, asking what my purpose is? Be thankful - there are those who did not live long enough to get the opportunity to think so.

> Remember, seven days without GOD makes one WEAK!!
>
> And without GOD, our week would be: Sinday, Mournday, Tearsday, Wasteday, Thirstday, Fightday and Shatterday.

Bibliography

- Bracey, Hyler Jack Rosenblum et.al,
  Aubrey Sanford & Roy Trueblood
  Managing From The Heart (1990)   ISBN No. 0-385-30425-0
- Brantley, Jeffrey and
  Wendy Millstine, *Five Good Minutes With The One You Love* (2007)
  New Harbinger Publications, Inc., USA
  ISBN No.-13:978-1-57224-512-9.
- Birx, Ellen Jikai and Charles Shinkai Rirx
  Waking Up Together (2005)
  Wisdom publications, Boston, USA   ISBN No. 0-86171-395-8
- Bushrui, Suheil,
  Gibran's Little Book of Love (2007)
  Oneworld Publications, England   ISBN No. 10: 1-85168-517-0
- Carlson, Richard and Benjamin Shield, ed.,
  Handbook for the Heart (1996)
  Little Brown and Company, USA   ISBN No. 0-316-12828-7
- Chopra, Deepak and David Simon
  The Seven Spiritual Laws of Yoga (2004)
  John Wiley & Sons, USA   ISBN No. 0-471-64764-0
- Chopra, Deepak, *The Path to Love* (1977),
  Harmony Books, New York, USA   ISBN No. 0-517-70622-9
- Cottlieb, Daniel
  Learning from the Heart (2008)
  Sterling Publishing Co., Inc. New York, USA
  ISBN No. 10-1-4027-4999-6
- Farhi, Donna, *Bringing Yoga to Life* (2003)
  Harper Collins Publishers, USA   ISBN No.0-06-009114-2
- Kolbell, Erik & Stephen M.Pollan
  Life Scripts (2002)
  Pocket Books, New York, USA   ISBN No. 0-7434-0060-7
- Pearsall, Paul, *The Heart's Code* (1998)
  Broadway Books, USA   ISBN No. 0-7679-0077-4
- Trehan B.K and Indu Trehan,
  Effective Yoga for Health and Happiness (2009),
  Macmillan Publishers India Ltd., India   ISBN No. 023-063-805-8